COOKING FOR THE CULTURE

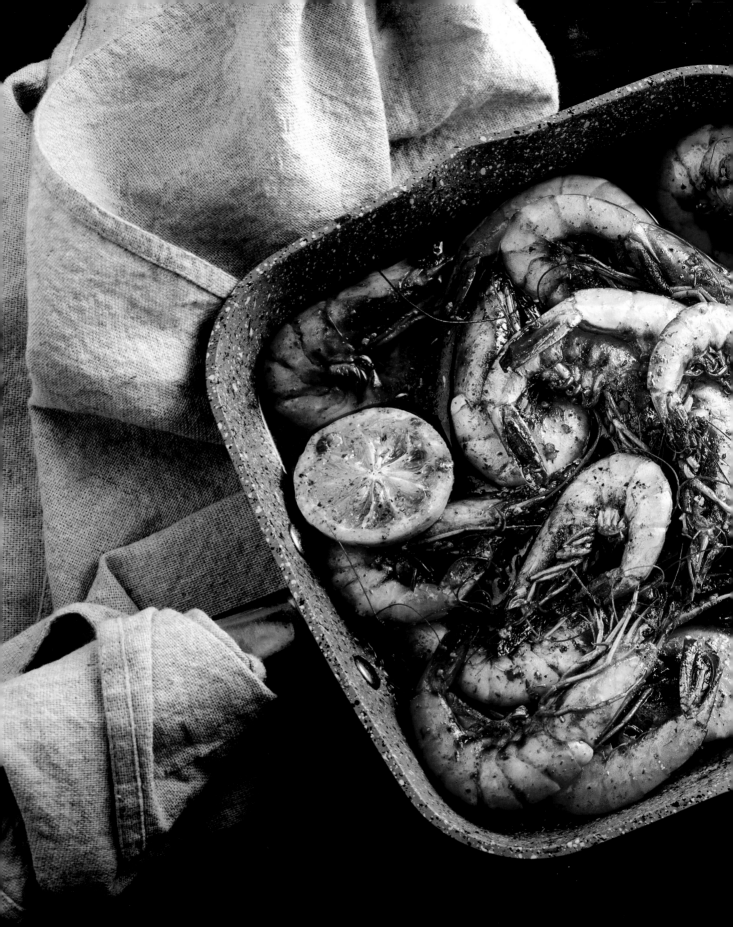

COOKING
FOR THE
CULTURE

Recipes and Stories from
the Streets of New Orleans
to the Table

TOYA BOUDY

Countryman Press

An Imprint of W. W. Norton & Company
Celebrating a Century of Independent Publishing

For information about permission to
reproduce selections from this book,
write to Permissions, Countryman Press,
500 Fifth Avenue, New York, NY 10110

For information about special discounts
for bulk purchases, please contact
W. W. Norton Special Sales at
specialsales@wwnorton.com
or 800-233-4830

Manufacturing by Chang Jiang Printing Media Co., Ltd.
Book design by Allison Chi
Production manager: Devon Zahn

Countryman Press
www.countrymanpress.com

An imprint of W. W. Norton & Company, Inc.
500 Fifth Avenue, New York, NY 10110
www.wwnorton.com

978-1-68268-745-1

10 9 8 7 6 5 4 3 2 1

To my best friend, my husband, and my manager, Christopher Boudy.

To my readers: I created this to be a peek over the fence into my life and journey up to now. I want this to ignite many fires inside of you. I want to be so transparent that it makes you crave to look deeper into yourself. I want my execution and creativity to knock the dust off a dream waiting. I want my words to stick with you, bubbling up when you need them most. I've always understood that this life is not my own. One of my missions is to light enough fires around the world so that the darkness won't seem as dark, won't be as scary. I intend for you to feel empowered, seen, and be well laced with ambition by the end of this book.

I invite you to follow my journey through food, black culture, life lessons, and art. Though everyone's journey is different, I hope by the end of this book, you are sparked to spread your wings, find your "why," heal, and feed people along the way.

Long live the dreams we have within.

CONTENTS

8 CHAPTER ONE.
BREAKFAST AND BRUNCH

10 Sweet Cream Farina

13 The Perfect Scramble

14 Southern Grits

15 Oven-Baked Bacon

16 Drop Biscuits with Blackberry Jam

19 Perfect Cup of Coffee

21 Bayou Brunch Po'boy

22 TOYA'S JOURNEY.
COOKING WITH CONFIDENCE

23 Sparkling Punch

27 Peanut Butter Cookies

28 Lemon Squares

30 Eggplant Parmesan

32 CHAPTER TWO.
SANDWICHES AND LIGHT MEALS

34 Eggs & Rice

37 Shrimp on Bun

38 Fried Chicken Kabob

41 Buttermilk Turkey Wings

42 Grilled Cheese 4 Ways

46 Chicken Salad

48 Fried Chicken & Watermelon Jam Sandwich

52 TOYA'S JOURNEY.
FOOD WAS A LOVE LANGUAGE

54 Liver & Onions

55 Chicken Noodle Soup

57 Collard Greens

58 French Fries 4 Ways

62 Pepperoni Lasagna

66 CHAPTER THREE.
MAINS

68 Fried Shrimp & Rocafella Cream

72 Jambalaya

75 Smothered Chicken

79 Seafood Gumbo

82 Stove-Top Seafood Boil

86 BBQ Shrimp

89 Chargrilled Oysters with Blue Crabmeat

93 Smothered Okra & Shrimp

95 Fried Fish

96 Fried Chicken

99 Ravioli

100 Baked Mac & Cheese

103 Yakamein

104 BBQ Salmon

107 Coconut Shrimp with Mango Chili Sauce

109 TOYA'S JOURNEY.
MAMA, I'M ON TV NOW

114 Classic Steak & Lobster

116 Fried Ravioli with Tasso Cream

119 Pancetta Pancakes

120 Bloody Mary Shrimp & Grits

123 Beignets with Raspberry Coulis

127 Browned Butter Scallops

129 Buttermilk-Roasted Chicken with Black Truffle Potatoes

131 Expensive Ass Salad

134 Crab Cakes with Lemon Caper Cream

137 Tartare 4 Ways

141 Expensive Ass Deviled Eggs

142 CHAPTER FOUR.
SIDES AND SOUP

144 Red Beans

147 Corn Bread

148 Cajun Corn on the Cob

153 Fried Okra

154 Succotash

156 Red Gravy

158 Crawfish Bisque

160 Sweet Potato Bisque

162 Potato Salad

163 Corn Bread & Black Bean Salsa

166 Lemon Pepper Green Beans

167 Cajun Smothered Potatoes

168 TOYA'S JOURNEY.
HOLIDAYS AT HOME

170 Stuffed Peppers

173 Christmas Chicken

174 Dressing 4 Ways

180 Bourbon Brown Sugar Spiral Ham

182 Black-Eyed Peas & Collard Greens

186 Endive Appetizers

189 Praline Bacon

190 Praline Sweet Potatoes with Whiskey Mallo Cream

193 Bourbon-Glazed Lamb Chops with Marinated Beans

196 CHAPTER FIVE.
SWEETS AND SIPS

199 Cookies & Cream Ice Cream

201 Strawberry Shortcake

205 Pumpkin Roll

208 7Up Cake

210 Peach Cobbler

211 White Chocolate Bread Pudding

214 Lavender Tea Cakes

217 Hurricane

218 Lemonade 4 Ways

225 Acknowledgments

227 Index

CHAPTER ONE

BREAKFAST AND BRUNCH

Early birds always get the worm

So much happened in the morning at my house, starting just before the sun arrived.

From bed I could smell coffee, something sizzling in the pan, and the sounds of the dog food being poured into a metal bowl while the Channel 4 news blared from the front room. Sometimes I'd wait to rise until I heard footsteps and saw the hall light peaking underneath my door, or other times I'd get up on my own to sit in the kitchen to watch my daddy pack his lunch for work—the lunch was so big that my uncle Walter called it a "Yogi Bear lunch." As my daddy was leaving for work, my mama would be coming home from working one of her jobs. Sometimes both of my parents held two jobs depending on the circumstances. Mornings weren't for lounging. They were for the getting ahead of the daily curves and turns of your daily work. There was a great deal of order to this time.

No one slept past 8 AM unless it was one of my parents sleeping to rest before an overnight shift, or if it was your birthday—and even then, my mama would be so excited that it was one of our birthdays that she would wake us up just to tell us "Happy Birthday." Needless to say, with all the work and constant daily routines, my sisters and I formed a firm work ethic. There's three of us, all girls, and my parents managed to never give any of us any kind of excuse or reason why we couldn't do something—not gender, time, money, or lack thereof for that matter. Not one thing was presented to us as if it wasn't possible.

Both of my parents are amazing cooks, both knew how to grill well, both could fix just about anything with their hands, and could even tell you what was wrong with your car if you drove up or started it up in front of them. They were a team. We really saw it at work when they made the decision to buy a house. Of course, everyone wants to buy a home, but it's always a certain "push" that gets them there. For us, it was someone attempting to break into our apartment. That was the last straw. You see, my daddy grew up in the Magnolia Projects and my mama shared a tight space with her five siblings Uptown, so they both had this engine inside them, driving them to get better for us. I remember the day they stood together and looked at the broken glass from the window. I knew something would be different simply because generally when they stood together, shit changed and the problem would be solved or fixed after that.

Often, I compliment them on how they made us so firm and loving just by leading by their actions. Both of them have type A personalities, and they've learned how to flow like a freshly tuned-up bicycle. They worked hard as hell, and they fought like any couple does and we'd see them fuss at each other, but then you'd see my mama get up out of her sleep to set the coffeepot to brew for my daddy like it was his alarm clock, waiting for him to get out of bed. And you'd see him fixing her something to eat or walking up behind her to kiss her on the cheek. Do I think they knew the strong and nurturing women they were creating? I don't think so. The more I've gotten to know them as adults, and not just parents, the more I've come to realize that they were just loving us the way they knew best—by leading, teaching, nurturing, and it was just that, the best they knew. They're the reason why we're all great artists and entrepreneurs. They taught us well.

SWEET CREAM FARINA

2 SERVINGS

Believe it or not, I remember getting ready for kindergarten vividly. Dark mornings, maybe 6 AM, freshly ironed clothes, super neat hair, and breakfast. Sounds impossible, doesn't it? Notice how early we got up when school started at 8:15 AM. Timing is key. As black parents, especially in the 1980s, my parents knew their children wouldn't be treated the same as children of the other races. So in order to make sure their children would not be targeted in any way, they made sure my sisters and I were super neat, pressed, and well behaved. It sent a direct message that said, "This kid is cared about." My parents were working hard, rotating shifts, and still finding time to make breakfast and iron. Food was made from scratch and the house was clean, no matter the hours they worked. Breakfast was warm and super comforting. My mama made farina so sweet you'd think, "This must be the stuff that put Goldie to sleep in baby bear's bed." There was always extra sweet milk around the edges. If love could be disguised as porridge it would be farina.

2 cups milk
¼ cup evaporated milk
1 pinch salt
4 tablespoons sugar
½ teaspoon vanilla extract
⅓ cup cream of wheat (farina)
Fresh fruit for topping
    (optional)

1   Bring both milks to a simmer over medium-high heat in a medium saucepan.

2   Add the salt, sugar, and vanilla extract. Heat until the sugar dissolves, stirring frequently.

3   Gradually add in the cream of wheat, stirring until it is completely incorporated. Use a whisk to smooth out any lumps that may occur.

4   Depending on the type of cream of wheat you use, there will be different cook times. Cook on low for the amount of time directed on the box.

5   Once done, remove from heat and serve. It can be topped with fresh fruit or enjoy it just the way it is!

THE PERFECT SCRAMBLE

As he was teaching me how to cook eggs, my dad told me, "They say if you can cook an egg, you can cook anything." My parents were very big on breakfast, and I swear it feels like everyone from New Orleans is the same way. You can pick up a quick $2.50 breakfast with a few faves, including eggs, bacon or hot sausage, and grits. You can find a plate anywhere, from Uptown to downtown.

8 eggs
½ cup milk
2 tablespoons butter
½ teaspoon salt, more to taste
½ teaspoon black pepper, more to taste
Optional toppings: minced herbs, shredded cheese, ¼ cup sautéed mushrooms, or chopped tomatoes

1 Crack open all the eggs into a medium bowl and begin to whisk until it goes from a deep yolk yellow to a lighter yellow.

2 Add the milk and get real whisk-y with it! Whisk by hand for 1 minute.

3 Heat a large nonstick skillet over medium-low heat, then add the butter and let it melt.

4 Once the butter starts to get a few bubbles, make sure that you tilt the skillet to make sure the butter coats the pan, then immediately add the eggs without stirring them. Sprinkle the salt and black pepper, then let them cook for 1 minute before scrambling them.

5 This is the time to add minced herbs, shredded cheese, sautéed mushrooms, chopped tomatoes, or anything else you like, or keep them plain.

6 Using a spatula or wooden spoon, gently scrape the edges, working your way to the center and folding them gently while breaking them apart and scrambling to form cloudlike eggs. Keep shifting them until all the liquid is gone, about 8 minutes, depending on how soft or firm you want them. Remember, they will continue to cook and set once they are off the heat.

SOUTHERN GRITS

6 SERVINGS

Grits is an all-day kinda thing, a dish my parents made a lot when I was younger. As an adult, I'd say that in the morning, it's good; in the afternoon, it's brunch; and late at night, it's a part of the recovery process from an exciting night out in the city. Stone-ground is the way to go, but you could "make it do what it do," with regular ole five-minute grits too. Don't trip, I add milk to my grits because it gives them a richer feel. But you can leave out the milk if you want. Either way you go, it'll be amazing.

6 cups water

2 cups milk

2 teaspoons salt, more if needed

½ teaspoon pepper

2 cups grits

2 tablespoons butter for serving

1 Add the water, milk, salt, and pepper to a medium pot. Begin to heat up over medium-high heat until you see steam rising from the liquid. If you wait for the boiling point, it will overflow because dairy rises, and even though only one-quarter of the liquid is dairy, it will still react the same.

2 Turn down the heat, and before the liquid begins to boil, quickly whisk or stir in all the dry grits and stir until you can tell the grits are beginning to absorb more liquid and begin to have a fuller look.

3 Put the lid on partially and stir occasionally until the grits are no longer gritty and hard, about 20 minutes.

4 Once the grits are tender, you can add the butter to the whole pot with extra salt or you can let everyone add what they like at the table.

OVEN-BAKED BACON

6 SERVINGS

There was nothing better than a bacon sandwich with mayonnaise when I was a kid. I'd cook the bacon in the microwave and knock out a pound in no time flat. Now, I know there are a few ways to make bacon, and if you're looking for that perfect shape, my absolute favorite method is to use the oven. I started doing this when I had my first catering job and served breakfast for a hundred people, and it was a total breeze! It's also good for saving the fat for later usage.

1 pound hickory smoked bacon

1 Preheat the oven to 400°F.

2 Line an 18-by-13-inch sheet pan with foil or parchment paper.

3 Arrange the bacon horizontally for the first full row; you'll notice you can only fit one column horizontally, so for the second add them vertically until the pan is completely full. I recommend laying the bacon like this to prevent you from having to do two rounds of bacon in the oven.

4 Bake them for 15 minutes, then flip them and bake for an additional 4 minutes. With this timing you'll have firm but not super crispy bacon. The bacon grease is terribly hot, so it will continue to cook in the hot grease if you leave it sitting. You can carefully remove them with a fork and line them up flat on a paper towel–lined plate to remove the grease by patting dry. Enjoy!

DROP BISCUITS WITH BLACKBERRY JAM

6 SERVINGS

These drop biscuits bring back warm memories. When I was a kid, I'd walk through the kitchen and spot fresh biscuits on the stove with the center dipped in where my mama had shoved a thick slice of butter. That buttery dip was the best part. You just break the biscuits in half and eat from the buttery center to the outer edges. My mother made the most beautiful drop biscuits, with perfect peaks and softness. In hindsight, I see it was just how she mothered me.

During the 2020 quarantine I was away from my parents for the longest time since Hurricane Katrina. Our family is super close, and our kids spend a lot of time with my parents. Hot biscuits and blackberry jam was the perfect breakfast to leave on the porch for them. My mama and daddy absolutely loved it and it did just what I intended it to do, it made them feel loved from afar.

FOR THE BISCUITS

2 cups self-rising flour
½ teaspoon salt
1½ cups heavy whipping cream
Butter for brushing

FOR THE JAM

1 teaspoon unsalted butter
1 cup sugar
5 cups fresh blackberries
2 teaspoons lemon juice

TO MAKE THE BISCUITS

1 Add the flour and salt to a medium bowl. Pour in the cream and stir with a wooden spoon until mixed. Preheat the oven to 475°F.

2 Dump out the contents of the bowl onto a counter and scrape out any remaining dough or flour. Pat into a rectangle about 2 inches thick. Fold in thirds, turn one-quarter and fold again, continuing three times, ending with a patting.

3 Cut the biscuits with a 3-inch biscuit cutter. Press it down into the dough and bring it straight up. Do not twist the biscuit cutter. Pat out the excess dough, cut, and repeat the process again.

4 Place the biscuits on a cookie sheet about 2 inches apart. Bake for 12 minutes, until golden. Brush with butter. Serve warm.

TO MAKE THE BLACKBERRY JAM

1 In a small pot, melt the butter over medium heat.

2 Add the sugar and blackberries and stir to prevent from sticking. As the mixture reaches a slight boil, lower the heat to low and allow it to thicken and dissolve the sugar. Continue to stir occasionally for 20 to 25 minutes.

3 After about 5 minutes, when the juices coat the back of the spoon without grit from the sugar, add the lemon juice, stir, and remove from the heat.

4 After cooling it will begin to become more of a jelly. You can always speed this process up by putting it in the freezer for about 20 minutes.

5 When the temperature is to your liking it's ready to serve. It will last roughly 2 weeks refrigerated.

PERFECT CUP OF COFFEE

6 SERVINGS

One day during hurricane season, the power was out at my parents' house so my middle sister, Elise, and I went to bring them a hot breakfast. I made the food and Elise made her "special coffee." We got to the house and Elise opened this huge fancy thermos canister and I was smacked with this beautiful spice- and nut-scented coffee. It tasted just as good as it smelled too! I swear, for once I thought, "I could drink this black, it's so smooth!" Try it and it'll be your new fall favorite.

¾ **cup coffee grounds**
6 cups water
¼ **teaspoon cinnamon**
¼ **teaspoon nutmeg**
1 pinch salt
Coffee syrup for serving (recipe follows)

1   Add the coffee grounds to your coffee maker as you normally would.

2   Add water to your coffee maker as you normally would.

3   Add the cinnamon, nutmeg, and salt to the coffee grounds.

4   Brew and enjoy the smell and flavor. Add a homemade syrup to shake things up a little.

HOMEMADE COFFEE SYRUP

MAKES ¾ CUP

Homemade coffee syrup is one of the easiest useful things you can make. This syrup takes 15 minutes to make and you can flavor it how you like. I look for any way to make my family feel special, and having little whatnots like this really adds the cherry on top! This would also make an amazing gift for neighbors or teachers. Premium coffee with a beautiful glass bottle of coffee syrup will brighten any moment.

¾ **cup water**
¾ **cup sugar**
1 tablespoon vanilla extract

1   Heat the water and sugar in a small saucepan until the sugar completely dissolves.

2   Remove from heat and add the vanilla, stir, and store up to 2 weeks in an airtight container refrigerated.

BAYOU BRUNCH PO'BOY

6 SMALL PO'BOYS

The first time I got paid for cooking was when I worked at a convenience store while in high school. I'd "auditioned" for the job by making a few dishes and bringing them around. I didn't realize it at the time but I discovered something I was good at—making food. One of the most popular sandwiches I'd make at the convenience store was the hot sausage po'boy on French bread. I decided to add a little razzle-dazzle to the original recipe to make it a brunch po'boy, because why not? It's super filling and absolutely perfect.

6 Patton's hot sausage patties (see Note) or other spicy sausage
6 large eggs
Cajun seasoning
Oil for cooking eggs
1 tablespoon butter
¼ cup chopped bell pepper
¼ cup chopped celery
½ cup chopped onion
1 (16-ounce) pack of crawfish tails with fat or raw deveined shrimp
1 loaf French bread, cut into 6-inch pieces

1 Fry the hot sausage patties using a large nonstick griddle or skillet until they're crispy on both sides, 6 to 7 minutes on each side, then drain on paper towels. Set aside.

2 In a large oiled cast-iron or ceramic skillet, add the eggs and sprinkle them with the Cajun seasoning to taste. I like to cook mine over hard, so when the whites are getting a little crispy, flip them. I personally like to tap the yolk so it can cook all the way through. You can do your eggs however you like! If you want them sunny-side up and runny, you can do it! Want them scrambled, you can do it! Set aside once all the eggs are cooked.

3 In a small skillet, add the butter and your chopped vegetables. Sauté for 8 to 10 minutes, or until caramelized over medium heat. Keep in mind the crawfish are completely cooked. We're just trying to flavor them properly. Add the crawfish with fat and season to taste with Cajun seasoning. Remove from the heat and get ready to assemble that sandwich.

4 Slice the patties in half lengthwise; use two halves per sandwich. Place them on the bread overlapping.

5 Add a couple of spoonfuls of eggs to each sandwich in a single layer.

6 Spoon on the crawfish mixture and serve.

NOTE: Patton's is a hot sausage brand used widely in the South and it can be purchased online. You can use the patties or links.

COOKING WITH CONFIDENCE

When I was a child, I loved cooking for my family, especially when my cousin Krystal was sitting at the countertop as if it was a bar.

I didn't know any chefs but I pretended to be one. I would wrap her sandwich in paper towels, taping them and writing her name on it as if it were a deli.

I never had a dream of what exactly I'd become. I had a craving to perform, even though there were no actors in the family and no one was even talking about the entertainment business. After watching a movie, I'd lock myself in the bathroom pretending in the mirror to accept awards or act out scenes. I listened to songs birthed more than a decade before me and visualized the music video.

These were clues to my future, but at that point of my life, I couldn't even be trusted in school to go to the restroom and return directly back to class. I didn't turn in homework either. I'd wait until the night before a project was due to start working on it. My parents really had a job on their hands with me. I didn't feel like I was capable of anything in school. Thankfully, I was always respectful. That was one thing I had going for me. Once a teacher who was known for being mean (now, as an adult, I know that it was classism and some racism) told my mama and the principal that I was disrespectful,

and that I left class to wander the halls. My mama quickly responded, "Now Toya may have left class and not come back, but I know she wasn't disrespectful to you, that's not her."

I'm sure you've gathered that I didn't have the best track record with school. Honestly, it began very early, and I'm talking preschool early. I got put out of preschool for trying to escape. The teacher caught me hanging out of the window; they called my mama to get me, and let her know that I wasn't able to return. More signs and hints that my path would be my own, more signs and clues that would let everyone know that my way would be paved by my steps and my steps alone.

Looking back I'm glad that I didn't have a view or idea of what I truly wanted to be. I would have done the same thing I did to the hall pass, namely abuse its purpose and the privileges that came along with it. Now I look back at my journey affectionately. As if it was boot camp for where I am now and where I am still traveling to. All of it trained me, built up muscles to handle the weight of the wisdom and understanding I now carry.

SPARKLING PUNCH

6 TO 8 SERVINGS

My cousin Krystal and I were very close, practically inseparable. She'd always be down for anything I wanted to make in the kitchen. We had this knack for making something out of nothing. In the 1990s, sparkling fruit-flavored water was super popular, but we wanted soda. My mama wasn't too big on juice or cold drinks (slang for soda). One day Krystal and I were in the kitchen and I came up with the idea to mix the sparkling water and sugar with Kool-Aid to make soda. You now see how serious I was about doing my own thing. If my mama didn't allow drinks like soda that often, and if I wanted it so bad, then I'd try to make it myself, right? So I made it and we both thought it was so good! Krystal looked at the cup and said, "I bet we can sell this," which is totally the dynamic of our personalities and how we fed each other's creativity and entrepreneurial spirits then, and still do until this day. We still inspire each other the same way, and this memory makes me smile when I look back at it because it reminds me that who we became wasn't a becoming, it was just something time and life had to reveal. We've always been creators and businesswomen. It was such a context clue, a beautifully crafted glimpse of the future.

2 liters strawberry-flavored sparkling water

1 (.23-ounce) packet strawberry Kool-Aid

1 cup sugar

1 bag (14 ounces) frozen sliced strawberries (optional)

1 Refrigerate the sparkling water overnight.

2 Mix the sparkling water, Kool-Aid, and sugar together carefully in a pitcher or a punch bowl.

3 Add the frozen strawberries, if using, to keep the mixture cool. Serve with ice.

The Luxury of Commodity Foods

Let me start with this: Summer is a taxing time for lower income families. Wanna know why? Those kids are home all day eating, drinking, running water, and cutting on lights. Seems like a normal thing, right? Nah, it ain't, because now the bills are higher and the amount of food in the cabinets is lower. During the school year the grocery bill handled breakfast and dinner, and you didn't have to worry about lunch because the school took care of that and classroom schedules didn't permit snacking. It meant you had to buy less food. But when summer hits, that meal plan is not going to work. As for the bills, it's the same thing. Kids running in and out of the house until mama yells, "You stay in or out! You're letting out all of the AC!"

My parents were both hard workers, but having a new house made things tighter. We were safer though, so it was a decent wash. Money was low during the summer, but we could never get any assistance because we were always right at the income limit. You had to make underneath a certain amount in order to qualify and with two hardworking parents in the household that was nearly impossible.

Despite that, my parents worked together and figured everything out, always. Someone shared commodity boxes with us, and for me it was like a creative Christmas. Commodity boxes were filled with government-issued foods to help families in need. A box contained cereal, dry milk, cheese, peanut butter, and a bunch of other items. I was excited not because I was so hungry, don't get it twisted—my mama cooked her ass off, everything from scratch, and all meals that stretched. I was excited because it was like a fresh pack of markers and paper to me.

One time when I was about 9, I was fumbling through a box and saw a large white can with an outline drawing of a peanut in the shell. Running my hands over the sides of the ridged can, I rotated it around and I saw a recipe for peanut butter cookies. In my head I went through the ingredients and thought, "We got that, that, we got that, this too, I'm gonna make this." I popped open the can and saw that oily surface. It immediately provoked me to stir it up until it was smooth. I remember the feeling I had when I first made the crisscross design with a fork on the cookies, and saw them baked all brown and beautiful. The first bite. I still feel that surge of victory. Little did I know that surge was like throwing coals into my eternal fire of creativity that would reveal itself later. Humble beginnings.

PEANUT BUTTER COOKIES

MAKES 2 DOZEN

No matter how you make it, whether it's commodity peanut butter (see page 25) with oil sitting at the top or a brand name standard, just about everyone has a story or memory tied to their childhood with peanut butter cookies. This cookie is number two, right after chocolate chip cookies. These are best eaten directly off the pan out of the oven. Burning your fingertips slightly is worth every moment after that first bite.

½ cup unsalted butter
½ cup smooth peanut butter
¼ cup brown sugar
½ cup granulated sugar
1 egg
2 teaspoons vanilla extract
¾ teaspoon baking soda
½ teaspoon salt
1 cup all-purpose flour

1 Preheat the oven to 325°F.

2 Using a mixer, beat the butter and peanut butter until well blended.

3 Add the sugars and continue to blend until nice and fluffy.

4 Add the egg and vanilla and mix well.

5 Now add the baking soda, salt, and flour and mix well.

6 Scoop a heaping tablespoon of dough and use your palms to make a ball. Once you make the ball, use a fork pressing two ways, one horizontally and another on top vertically, making the crisscross pattern.

7 Bake them 2 inches apart on a parchment-lined sheet pan for 8 to 10 minutes, until the edges are set. Carefully lift the parchment paper to remove the cookies from the pan to cool on the countertop, otherwise the cookies will continue to cook on the baking pan when they come out of the oven. You don't want the edges to be brown unless you like crunchy cookies. Enjoy them warm or cool.

LEMON SQUARES

MAKES ONE 13-BY-9-INCH BAKING PAN

As a kid, in addition to making cookies I tried my hand at baking a few pastries. Lemon squares were one of them. I chose lemon squares because we always had lemons in the house. (Sometimes before my mama's shift she'd ask me to fill her water bottle up with fresh lemonade so she could sip on it throughout the night.) I chose what I was going to try to make primarily around what was in the cabinet or fridge. My mother still blames me for her weight gain. I used to wake her up out of a deep sleep to get her opinion on my lemon squares before she dozed back off until her 7 PM to 7 AM shift at the hospital.

FOR THE CRUST

2 cups plus 2 tablespoons all-purpose flour
1 cup powdered sugar
½ teaspoon salt
1 cup unsalted butter, melted
1 teaspoon vanilla extract

FOR THE FILLING

2½ cups granulated sugar
½ cup all-purpose flour
7 large eggs
1 cup lemon juice (store-bought is fine)
Pinch salt
Powdered sugar for dusting

TO MAKE THE CRUST

1 Preheat the oven to 350°F and line the bottom and sides of a 9-by-13-inch baking pan with parchment paper that sticks up above the sides of the pan, so that you can remove the bars later for easy cutting. Set pan aside.

2 Combine the flour, powdered sugar, and salt in a medium bowl.

3 Add the melted butter and vanilla extract and stir to combine completely.

4 Crumble and distribute over the bottom of the pan and press evenly into the bottom so that it's even.

5 Bake for 15 to 20 minutes, until the edges are just getting lightly browned. Remove from oven and set aside.

TO MAKE THE FILLING

1 Combine the sugar and flour. Add the eggs, lemon juice, and salt and whisk together to combine. Don't overmix.

2 Pour the filling on top of the crust and bake for 18 to 22 minutes, until relatively set. Remove from the oven and cool for 15 to 20 minutes on the counter, then refrigerate until cold and firm.

3 Grab the ends of the parchment paper and carefully lift the bars from the pan. Dust with powdered sugar, then cut into squares right before serving. They'll last 5 days in the refrigerator.

EGGPLANT PARMESAN

6 SERVINGS

Sometimes I wanted to cook when I was growing up, and sometimes there was too much going on in my life. I remember one time, when I was about 17, I dusted off my cookbook and decided to try something toward the "back of the book," which had what I thought were the harder recipes. I flipped it open to "Eggplant Parmesan." I never had it before, so I read through the recipe and thought, "I think I can do this." And guess what? I did it well. It was the first meal that got a real compliment from my daddy. He gave me "the look" all cooks want to see after the first bite . . . the "damn this is good" look. I felt tall that day. I expanded my own palate and I never turned back . . .

2 medium to large eggplants

1 tablespoon plus 1 teaspoon salt

1½ cups bread crumbs

¼ cup grated Parmesan cheese

½ teaspoon pepper

2 teaspoons Italian seasoning

1 cup flour

2 large eggs

1 tablespoon milk

¼ cup canola oil, more as needed

1 (24-ounce) jar marinara sauce, but if you want to be saucy, use 2 (24-ounce) jars

8 ounces mozzarella cheese, freshly grated

Fresh basil for garnish

1 Slice the eggplant into ¼-inch-thick slices and place on baking sheet(s) in an even layer. Sprinkle 1 tablespoon of the salt all over the eggplant slices and let rest for 60 minutes.

2 In a shallow bowl, mix together the bread crumbs, Parmesan cheese, 1 teaspoon salt, pepper, and Italian seasoning. Place the flour in another shallow bowl. Whisk the eggs and milk in a third shallow bowl. Place the bowls in this order to make it all easier: flour, eggs, and bread crumb mixture.

3 Rinse the eggplant slices in a colander and then pat dry with paper towels.

4 Preheat the oven to 400°F.

5 Bread the eggplant: dip in the flour first, then in the egg, and last in the bread crumb mixture. Place the eggplant slices on a clean baking sheet.

6 Pan-fry the eggplant: Heat 2 to 3 tablespoons canola oil in a large nonstick frying pan over medium-high heat. Once hot and shimmering, add in the eggplant slices using tongs. Don't overcrowd the pan, only fit as many as you can in an even layer.

7 Fry until golden brown, 4 to 5 minutes on each side. Add more oil to the pan as needed in between batches. Place the fried eggplant on paper towel–lined baking sheets.

8 Layer the eggplant slices in an even layer in a 13-by-9-inch baking dish. Pour 12 ounces of the marinara sauce over the layer of eggplant. Then add another layer of eggplant slices over that, followed

by the remaining 12 ounces marinara sauce. If you want to be extra saucy, add more marinara sauce as you see fit. Top with the shredded mozzarella cheese and bake for 20 to 25 minutes. Broil for 2 to 3 minutes (optional).

9 Let rest for at least 15 minutes and garnish with basil. Enjoy with more marinara, as desired.

CHAPTER TWO

SANDWICHES AND LIGHT MEALS

Black ingenuity shows up in the kitchen

From nothing to something, and from little we make more.

My parents never harped on gender roles and that was always interesting to me. It was never ever said, "A woman should cook." It was more of a common sense framing like, "You gotta eat right? You better cook." My parents made everything from scratch, always meals that stretched, and rarely did we eat boxed or fast-food meals. I used to think it was because my mother was against any other food, until I got old enough to truly understand a statement that has been so famously said in black households: "You got McDonald's money?"

When I experienced life enough to know, I understood it was cheaper to take a $6 pack of chicken, smother it with gravy, serve it over rice, and eat that for two to three days versus getting a sack of fast food or buying boxed Hamburger Helper, which would only last one night. Money and food had to stretch, especially when both parents worked hard each day. And don't talk about having *too* much left over on the second day, because it could be frozen to be used another time.

It's the brilliance born in moments of survival that wows me. The brilliance is within the strategy, the stretch, and the timing. This has been in our ancestral repertoire since before slavery but, for sure, being thrown scraps heightened it. Low money? Basics in the cabinet? You could eat for two weeks off $25 or less. Don't talk about if you have

dirt and sunlight . . . my friend, you're rich—you have a garden. Now, what's seen as lack with one head tilt can, with another tilt, become a blank canvas for endless opportunities. That relentless drive to have what's needed keeps the ideas flowing.

I believe you only need to have a few techniques under your belt, all about how to make filling dishes or utilizing stretching techniques. Learn how to smother something, which takes roux knowledge. If you know how to make a roux, then you essentially know how to make gumbo, gravies, béchamel, and stews, and you have the ability to take a meal that would feed two people and stretch it to six. If you can sauté veggies, then you can put that on top of rice. The drippings from a protein also go well over rice with butter, salt, and pepper. And, oh my word, don't forget about fried eggs with rice, or how we affectionately call it: New Orleanian "Eggs & Rice" (page 34). On nights we didn't want leftovers, or maybe for lunch, one of us would make eggs and rice. Come home from a late night? Hungry? Fry up a piece of sausage to go with the eggs and rice, and it will have you sleeping like a baby. Though these meals derived from moments that seemed like lack, they can nurture us now, and remind us of what we learned back then. It may seem like I have less, but I really have more.

EGGS & RICE

SERVES 3

Any local who grew up in the 1980s and '90s would agree that Eggs & Rice is a quick kitchen gem. If you didn't want to eat what was cooked, or if you didn't feel like making a sandwich, you made Eggs & Rice. My mom always kept a Pyrex dish filled with cooked rice because we ate a lot of meals with rice and then half the job was already done. I loved getting creative as a kid, adding green onions or cut-up pieces of luncheon meat if I was feeling fancy-schmancy. But the original is my favorite. Even now I'll make a big pan and it's something everyone's always in the mood for, day or night.

**3 tablespoons salted butter,
more if needed**
¼ cup chopped green onions
4 eggs
1 tablespoon milk
4 cups cooked rice
Salt and pepper to taste
**Cajun or Creole seasoning
(optional)**

1   Melt the butter over medium heat in a large skillet and add the green onions. Sauté until fragrant, about 5 minutes.

2   Meanwhile, whisk the eggs and milk in a bowl. Add to the butter and onions in the skillet and begin to scramble.

3   Halfway through being done, add the rice and begin to scramble them all together until the eggs are fully cooked. This should take 6 to 7 minutes to make sure the rest of the egg is cooked and the rice is fully heated.

4   Season to taste with salt and pepper or Cajun seasoning, if using. You can also add extra butter if you like at the end; that's fine too! Serve and enjoy!

My parents, the picture of black ingenuity

SHRIMP ON BUN

MAKES 4

Any day of the week you can hit me with a shrimp on bun. Breaded and fried, not too much jazz beyond that. I don't even need it fully dressed, just ketchup and pickles with a hot bun. It is an instant classic.

I worked at a corner store as a kid, and this was one of the dishes I enjoyed cooking and eating. Some of those recipes I kept simple, while some I added a flair, which I add to my own when I revisit them today. Shrimp on bun is one of the classics that you'll crave if you've moved away from New Orleans, and one of the ones that locals tell New Orleans newbies to try.

1 pound jumbo shrimp, peeled and deveined
½ teaspoon salt
1 teaspoon black pepper
1 teaspoon garlic powder
1 cup buttermilk
2 cups all-purpose flour
1 cup cornstarch
2 tablespoons smoked paprika
2 tablespoons Cajun seasoning
4 cups vegetable oil for frying
Brioche hamburger buns
Butter for buns
Ketchup and pickles for serving

1 Place the shrimp in a large bowl and toss lightly with salt, pepper, and garlic powder. Set aside. In another bowl, pour the buttermilk.

2 Mix the flour, cornstarch, paprika, and Cajun seasoning together in a shallow dish.

3 Line a baking sheet and set aside. One at a time, dip the shrimp in the buttermilk and dredge in the flour mixture. Shake off the excess flour and place the shrimp on the baking sheet.

4 Add the oil to a large skillet you're comfortable frying in, deep enough so you can fry the shrimp. Allow the oil to get up to 350°F, or until you see the ripples at the bottom of the pan.

5 Fry the shrimp a few at a time, 2 to 3 minutes, until golden brown. Drain on a plate lined with paper towels.

6 Toast and butter the brioche buns and begin to assemble the sandwiches. You can eat a sandwich plain with just shrimp and buttered buns or you can add ketchup and pickles.

FRIED CHICKEN KABOB

4 SERVINGS

This is something you never knew that you needed. I learned how to make these at the store and knew they were always selling out, but I didn't see what the hype was about because I never tried it. Once I did, I thought, "Ohhh, now I get it! It's that damn good! The flavor!" And honestly, so many things are more exciting on a stick or deep fried. This one hits both marks beautifully. I can still knock down two to three of these at a time, and they never get old to me.

2½ cups flour

1½ cups cornstarch

3 tablespoons Cajun seasoning, more for sprinkling directly onto chicken

1 tablespoon paprika

1 egg

1½ cups milk

2 large boneless chicken breasts cut into 1½-to-2-inch chunks

2 bell peppers, deseeded and cut into chunks

1 large onion, peeled and cut into chunks

1 (14-ounce) smoked sausage link, cut into 1½-inch chunks

1 quart oil for frying

8 to 10 wooden kabob skewers

1   Set up a dredging station. Mix the flour, cornstarch, 3 tablespoons Cajun seasoning, and paprika on a plate or a flat container. Next, mix the egg and milk in a medium bowl. Last, set up a plate or pan lined with paper towels, which will allow the kabobs to drain when finished frying.

2   Sprinkle the chicken chunks with Cajun seasoning.

3   Assemble the kabobs starting with a bell pepper chunk, then onion, chicken, and sausage. Then repeat and end with the bell pepper. I always cut my kabob skewers in half because it's a pretty hearty amount of ingredients on the kabob and I've noticed eating one does the trick for someone most times. Also, they're easier to fry when shorter if you're not using a deep fryer.

4   Dip the kabob in the flour mixture first, next dip in the egg mixture, then back in the flour mixture. This will make them extra crispy.

5   Fry in a large skillet over medium-high heat (the oil should reach a temp of 375°F) until golden for 4 minutes on each side, then drain them on the paper towels.

6   Serve while hot. Reheat in the oven at 450°F.

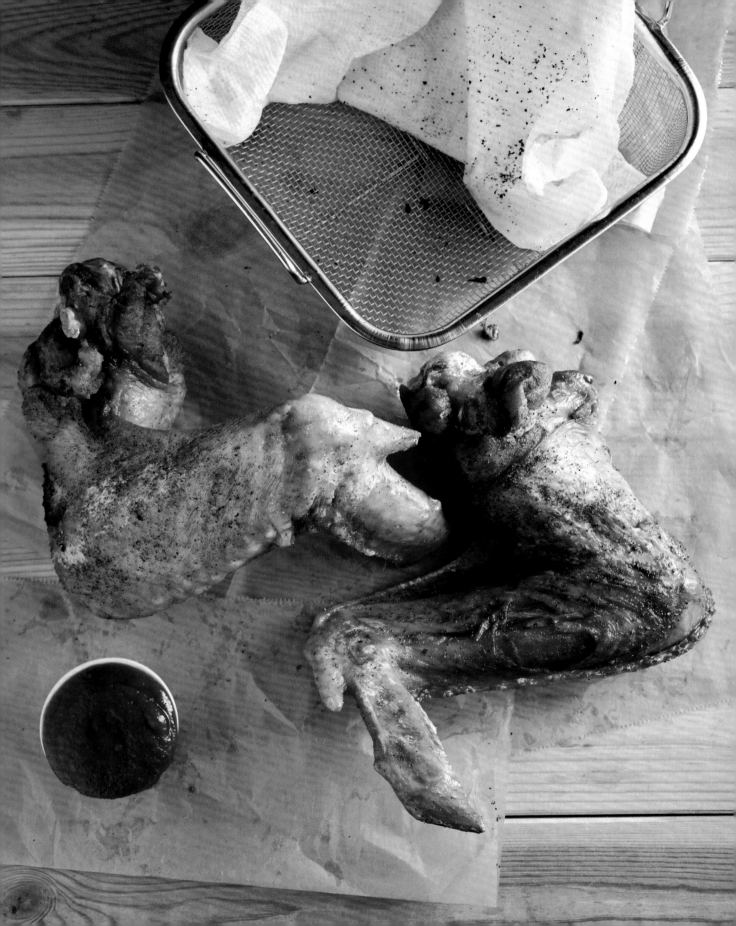

BUTTERMILK TURKEY WINGS

MAKES 4 WINGS

Believe it or not, fried turkey wings were something you could find in a corner store Uptown that my aunt Denise's friend Sheryl Ann worked in. And boy could she throw down with the best of them. Everything was good from that store because she ran the show and the kitchen. Sometimes when we were leaving from a visit to my grandparents and Aunt Denise's house, we'd pass through there to grab a bite before hitting the bridge to go to home. This was one of the things I loved most. I believe us frying turkey wings here in New Orleans, as well as us locals smothering turkey necks in gravy and eating them with rice, is just another testament to how we will leave no part behind when it comes to eating and especially frying. Here's a juicy rendition of those wings.

4 turkey wings, roughly 2 pounds depending on the size
4 cups buttermilk
2 tablespoons smoked paprika
½ teaspoon sage
2 garlic cloves, minced
2 tablespoons coarse salt
Cajun seasoning
Vegetable oil for frying

1 Add the turkey wings, buttermilk, paprika, sage, garlic, and salt into a large ziplock bag. Shift it around so everything can be mixed well, then refrigerate overnight.

2 When you're ready to cook them, sit the bag on the countertop to bring it to room temperature (this will help it cook evenly).

3 Remove the wings from the milk and lay them on a plate. Discard the leftover marinade. Pat them dry and sprinkle Cajun seasoning evenly over the wings.

4 In a deep fryer add enough oil to cover the wings. Heat up the oil to 375°F, because as soon as you add the wings it will drop to 350°F.

5 Deep-fry the wings until they're brown and cooked through, about 14 minutes.

6 Drain on paper towels. Serve hot!

GRILLED CHEESE 4 WAYS

In elementary school, I remember asking to go to the bathroom just to walk around the school. Yes, I would walk around just to take a little breather, and of course that was against the rules. Well, one of the rounds I would make was to pass around my friend's class to say hi through the window of the door, but before going back to class I'd pass around the cafeteria to see what was on the menu for the day. This was a deciding factor for how the rest of the school day would play out. I'd rubberneck to see into the slot of a window in the cafeteria doors, and if I saw the words "gumbo and grilled cheese," I'd feel a surge of excitement. I knew that the remainder of the day would be good, and that lunch would be eaten down to the last drop and crumb. I still to this day love grilled cheese with gumbo, and it's a must-have in my home.

As a child I wanted my grilled cheese plain, but there are so many possibilities with toasted buttery bread with hot cheese in the center accompanied by seafood, veggies, meat, or other cheeses. You can't go wrong; you can only go right!

SIMPLE GRILLED CHEESE

MAKES 2 SANDWICHES

1 teaspoon mayonnaise
4 slices Texas toast bread
6 slices American cheese
2 tablespoons salted butter

1   Assemble the sandwiches: each sandwich will have ½ teaspoon mayonnaise on one slice of bread, add the cheese on top of the mayo, and place the other slice of bread on top. The mayo adds a smooth creamy feel to the cheese once it melts.

2   Melt 1 tablespoon of the butter in a large cast-iron skillet over medium-high heat, then place both sandwiches in the skillet. Cook on one side until it's a beautiful golden color.

3   Remove the sandwiches from the skillet for a few seconds to add the last tablespoon of butter to the pan; once that melts add the sandwiches back so you can toast the other side.

4   Let them sit for 3 minutes then enjoy!

CRAWFISH GRILLED CHEESE

MAKES 4 SANDWICHES

5 teaspoons salted butter
3 green onions, chopped
½ teaspoon minced garlic
1 pound crawfish tails with fat, already cooked
1 teaspoon Cajun seasoning
8 slices Texas toast bread
8 slices Cheddar
4 slices pepper Jack

1   Melt 1 teaspoon of the butter; sauté the green onions and garlic until fragrant, about 5 minutes.

2   Add the crawfish tails and Cajun seasoning and sauté for 2 minutes just to blend the flavors. Remove from heat and set aside. Remember, the crawfish is fully cooked.

3   Assemble the sandwiches in the following order: 1 slice of bread, 2 slices of Cheddar, spoon about 3 tablespoons of crawfish mixture, 1 slice of pepper Jack on top of the crawfish, then the final slice of bread.

4   Assemble two sandwiches at a time unless you're using a griddle and can cook them all at once. You don't want to prep them ahead if you're not doing them at once because the crawfish could begin to wet the bread and it won't have that crispy toast feel we're going for.

CONTINUES

5 Over medium heat, melt ½ teaspoon of butter in a large cast-iron skillet for each sandwich, place the sandwiches in the pan, and cook until the first side is golden. Gently remove from the pan, melt another ½ teaspoon of butter for each sandwich, then cook the other side of the sandwich until golden as well. Repeat the process until you've done them all. Let them sit for 3 minutes then enjoy!

SPINACH AND ARTICHOKE GRILLED CHEESE

MAKES 4 SANDWICHES

4 ounces artichoke hearts
4½ teaspoons butter
1 teaspoon minced garlic
Cracked salt and pepper
8 slices Texas toast
4 slices provolone
4 slices mozzarella
1 cup chopped fresh spinach
4 slices pepper Jack

1 Add the artichokes to a bowl and break them apart, rinse them, and squeeze out the excess water and set aside.

2 Melt ½ teaspoon of the butter in a large cast-iron skillet, sauté the artichokes and garlic until fragrant, about 5 minutes. Salt and pepper to taste.

3 Assemble the sandwiches in the following order: 1 slice of bread, 1 slice each of provolone and mozzarella, spread about 1 tablespoon of artichoke mixture, ¼ cup chopped spinach, 1 slice pepper Jack on top of the spinach and artichokes, and then the final slice of bread.

4 Assemble two sandwiches at a time unless you're using a griddle and can cook them all at once. You don't want to prep them ahead if you're not doing them at once because the artichokes could begin to wet the bread and it won't have that crispy toast feel we're going for.

5 Over medium heat in a large cast-iron skillet, melt ½ teaspoon of the butter for each sandwich, cook until the first side is golden, and gently remove from the pan. Melt another ½ teaspoon for each sandwich, then cook the other side of the sandwich until golden as well. Repeat the process until you've done them all. Let them sit for 3 minutes then enjoy!

CRÈME DE LA CRÈME GRILLED CHEESE

4 SERVINGS

1 teaspoon olive oil
1 garlic clove, freshly chopped
¼ teaspoon salt
3 tablespoons mayo
8 slices Texas toast
4 slices mozzarella
4 slices Swiss
4 slices provolone
4 ounces whipped cream cheese
Cracked pepper
4 teaspoons butter

1 Add the olive oil, garlic, and salt to a small skillet, sauté over medium heat for 5 minutes until fragrant.

2 Mix the garlic mixture with the mayo and set aside.

3 Assemble the sandwiches in this order: Each sandwich will have a teaspoon of the garlic mayo spread evenly on 1 slice of bread, then begin layering the cheese on top of the mayo. First mozzarella, next Swiss, provolone, then spread the whipped cream cheese. Top with cracked pepper and then place the other slice of bread on top. We're cooking two sandwiches at a time.

4 Melt 1 teaspoon of butter over medium heat in a large cast-iron skillet, then place the sandwiches in the skillet. Cook on one side until it's a beautiful golden color.

5 Remove the sandwiches from the skillet for a few seconds to add the last teaspoon of butter to the pan, then add the sandwiches back so you can toast the other side. Repeat the process until all sandwiches are made.

6 Let them sit for 3 minutes then enjoy!

CHICKEN SALAD

6 SERVINGS

Our mama didn't play about leftovers. If three days passed and there was a portion of food left, she'd freeze it no matter how small. It's either getting frozen or it's getting repurposed for a dinner sequel that will cause us to finish the meal completely. Baked chicken, sherry chicken, you better believe that anything left over was going to be a chicken salad. Even if it was only enough chicken to make a single serving, she would make it. Often we'd joke about walking in the house like, "Damn! What's that?! You have more?" Only for her to respond and say, "It was only enough for me." We'd cackle about it, but now I see that she was making sure that none of the food went to waste because, after all, it wasn't free. She's so mindful and wise. I can see her in my mind right now, sitting on the couch, feet crossed, watching an episode of The Young and the Restless. *My mom had the VCR set up to record the soap operas that she would miss each day because of her work shift. Club crackers and chicken salad on the plate with an ice-cold 7Up, which was her favorite drink—and she was the only one allowed to drink it. Me opening the door after school and seeing her first thing, looking up to the left to greet me. Such a sweet and comforting memory that makes me look back affectionately over the past and smile.*

**2 cups leftover chicken breasts,
   cooked and shredded**
1 cup mayonnaise
½ teaspoon sugar
⅓ cup diced celery
⅓ cup sweet pickle relish
¼ teaspoon pepper
1 hard-boiled egg, minced
1 teaspoon smoked paprika
1 teaspoon salt

Mix together all the ingredients.

NOTE: You can toast bread and make a sandwich, you can make a wrap with lettuce, or enjoy with crackers.

FRIED CHICKEN & WATERMELON JAM SANDWICH

MAKES 4 SANDWICHES WITH LEFTOVER JAM

When I found out the root of a lot of judgments that were passed on black people regarding watermelons and fried chicken, I dug in to find the beauty that came before the mockery. I discovered that watermelon is a majestic fruit that grows easily in soil up to 85 percent sand, and has tons of health benefits. As for frying chicken, it came over with their techniques of braising chicken from their own cuisines. The West African slaves were forced to work in the kitchens where they then perfected one of America's most favorite dishes, fried chicken. Now I don't think of those ridiculously ignorant cartoons. Instead, I think of the land we originally came from with ground so fertile that even the sand can produce great fruit, and of minds and hands so gifted that in the worst of times edible icons can be produced. It only made perfect sense to combine these two as an ode to a flipped narrative, and for chucking a deuce to the mockery. Fried chicken and watermelon will forever be my jam.

FOR THE WATERMELON JAM

2 cups pureed watermelon
¼ cup fresh lemon juice
2 cups white sugar
2½ (6-ounce) packages powdered pectin
½ teaspoon crushed red pepper (optional)

FOR THE FRIED CHICKEN

4 boneless, skinless chicken thighs
½ cup buttermilk
1 teaspoon hot sauce
1 tablespoon plus 1 teaspoon kosher salt
Canola oil for frying
1½ cups all-purpose flour

1 teaspoon freshly cracked black pepper
2 teaspoons garlic powder
2 teaspoons smoked paprika
4 buns

TO MAKE THE WATERMELON JAM

1 Put the pureed watermelon, lemon juice, and sugar in a medium pot. Bring to a rolling boil, then reduce heat to a simmer.

2 Add the pectin and whisk it with a handheld whisk or a fork immediately, so it dissolves without clumping. Bring the watermelon jam to a boil again, add the crushed peppers, if using, and then reduce heat to a simmer. Simmer, stirring every minute, for 20 minutes.

3 Pour the watermelon jam into a pretty jar or other glass container. This watermelon jam will set completely once it's cooled. Refrigerate and use within a week.

TO MAKE THE FRIED CHICKEN

1 Add the chicken, buttermilk, hot sauce, and 1 teaspoon of the salt to a large resealable bag and refrigerate for at least 4 hours or up to overnight.

2 Heat 1½ inches of canola oil in a Dutch oven or large pot to 350°F.

3 In a wide bowl, combine the flour, remaining salt, pepper, garlic powder, and smoked paprika. Remove the chicken from the buttermilk marinade and dip each piece in the flour mixture until well coated. Place on a plate, so that when it's time to fry, everything feels like an assembly line.

4 Fry the chicken until golden brown and cooked through, about 4 minutes per side. Don't crowd the chicken in the pan, so work in two batches if necessary. Rest the cooked chicken on paper towels to cool.

5 Toast the buns.

6 Assemble by adding the chicken to a toasted bun and drizzle with watermelon jam.

Watermelon

There's ridicule and mockery attached to black people when it comes to fried chicken and watermelon. It started from a dark source. So dark that when I told my mama about the photo idea of me gripping watermelon she looked at me and said, "No, Toya." And I said, "Ma, I'm in a place creatively where I just want to take everything back that was used to make fun of us as black people or used to classify us as the lesser race." We've endured slurs in every form, even with the food that we make or enjoy. Watermelon used to be called nigger candy, and was often depicted as eaten by black people drawn as pickaninny characters. Pickaninnies had bulging eyes, kinky hair, and big red lips. They were shown eating huge slices of watermelon. They were portrayed as nameless, shiftless natural buffoons running from alligators and toward fried chicken.

Watermelon was one of the things that made it here during the slave trade, and it was widely popular in Africa because of its ability to feed and hydrate. The slave traders knew that the Africans' diet was a big part of our strength and health, and the traders needed them to be able to stay alive enough to work the land. Slave owners would allow some of the slaves to grow their own food, and watermelon was one of the things. It took a dark turn when slaves were emancipated: It seemed like anything the freed slaves did put them up for mockery. What they ate, looked like, wore, or even the way they spoke was mocked simply because of the anger former slave owners had, because the slaves had freedom.

FOOD WAS A LOVE LANGUAGE

From 6th grade to 12th grade, I spent every summer in summer school.

The summer after 9th grade was different from the rest for many reasons, one of them being that my mama told me that I needed to pay for it if I wanted to go. Also, I was on my way to the 10th grade that fall so I had a whole new world of high school waiting for me. Now let me be clear, because it may seem as if going to summer school was something I just wanted to do to pass the time; it wasn't, and my mother caught on to the trend.

By making me pay, I think she hoped I'd do better during the school year. Here's what would happen: I'd fail math every quarter, then go to school for a few weeks in the summer, and pass with a D. I know that seems backward, but you don't know the fear and insecurities I had centered on math. I legitimately thought that I wasn't capable, and summer school math was easier to pass because it wasn't based on months of passed tests and homework turned in on time. I guess that was my first stab at strategizing in order to make it through something.

Well, back to the summer of 1998 changing my life. I told my mama I was trying to find a job, and because she's very good at one liners, she said something that rang through me: "That's good you need to work, because the rate you're going, you're going to need to know how to work hard." Whew.

She's heavy, huh? She was right as always. I knew I could cook, so at 15 years old, I made a meal and went to two of the nearby corner stores with a plate of food hoping they would be wowed and hire me. I remember when I dropped the plates off, I skipped home. No lie, it was pure joy and excitement. It was chicken breast with diced tomatoes and pasta. Back then everything I made had way too much spice, I remember that much at least. It was a rush because I got to cook at home, but it wasn't full large meals or damn near catering like working at a corner store turned out to be. But I thought of all the food I'd eaten, like fried chicken and po'boys, I figured I'd catch on. It couldn't be harder than algebra.

Days after dropping the plate off, my phone rings and it's the store owner of the second store. He wanted me to cook and sometimes work as a cashier. I would make $200 every week, so that would quickly pay off summer school and also give me play money. Mission accomplished.

I'm sure you're wondering what in the hell could a 15-year-old cook in a corner store? In New Orleans, our corner stores have fried chicken, meat pies, po'boys, sliced deli meat, hog head cheese, and various produce items. Don't forget T-shirts, jewelry, mini bongs, chargers, supplies for a quick car tune-up, and just about anything you could probably throw in the mix—they'd have it. The workers become family to the community they serve. They know the daily ins and outs, they know which cigarettes a customer loves: "box or soft pack." Kool Filter Kings was a best seller, and so were Swisher Sweets singles. That was the summer I had the most freedom. Though I went to summer school, I worked, made money, and spent money just as fast. Paid on Sunday, broke on Monday.

Once summer school was over I was still allowed to work. But the rest of the summer was aimless for me, and I got involved with the wrong person. I wasn't one of those girls who guys liked much at all or even noticed for that matter. I was a 15-year-old girl who never did well in school, got picked on for the shoes I wore or the clothes I didn't have. And the worst of all to a teenager, to frost one of the toughest cakes in the world, boys ignored me. The grown men who came into the store did notice me. I thought they were "my type." I was wrong and my mama was right: Those men didn't see me, they just wanted one thing from me.

School started and I was still allowed to work after school. Finally, I could buy cool shoes for myself and a couple of cool outfits. I really felt like the 10th grade was going to be like turning a new leaf. On September 21, 1998 (the day before my 16th birthday) during my shift, my dad came in the store and asked me what was wrong. I said, "Nothing really, but this chicken grease is making me nauseous." And he said, "Really?" He looked concerned and left. I walked home that night. I remember how still it was, because I was always keeping an eye out for my surroundings. Approaching the door at home, I could see the bright lights on in the room when normally they'd only have the lamp on late at night. As soon as I got in my mama called me in the room. I thought something must be wrong. She jumped straight to the point: "Do you think you're pregnant?" My immediate response was, "I don't

know." She said, "Shit." She went directly to the store, and at this point it all feels like a blink. I take the test and instantly all of our lives are different.

In that moment I knew that 15-year-old me, who felt insignificant, has now done something so significant that no one near me would see me or maybe themselves the same again. The next day was my sweet 16th birthday, and guess where I was? Planned Parenthood, finding out that I was officially pregnant and being informed of "options" that I had and didn't know even existed. I still remember the look on my parents' faces. They worked so hard to keep me away from a hard life, and yet I walked directly onto a path that was one of the toughest ones, being a teenage parent. You have to know by this point I was constantly failing with what my mama called "doing fine grades," meaning Ds and Fs, and getting suspended way too often. Any adult who looked at me didn't have much hope for me before, so this sealed the deal in their minds. When I got the job I felt like I did something right in an offbeat way. Getting a job to pay for my mistakes and even being less of a burden, because I wasn't always asking for something. I felt like I messed things up more.

A lot of things changed immediately: my daddy called the store and told them I wasn't coming back. All of that famous teenage know-it-all was knocked out of me. I forever knew that I didn't know what I thought I did, and that my parents were warning me about life and knew me better than I knew myself. Looking back, it was the catalyst that jumpstarted my drive. Somehow, I finally began to see past "now." This person I've never met inside of me was valuable. This baby was now a reason in a world where I felt that all I did was cause trouble at home, and at school no one liked me. But now? I thought to myself, "I'll keep walking and I'll see where this goes." I had no plan outside of staying alive; little did I know how far I'd go.

LIVER & ONIONS

4 SERVINGS

While I was pregnant, I struggled with trying to keep up with the vitamins that the baby needed. I remember things were still quiet between my mama and me, and my dad was offshore the majority of the pregnancy for two reasons: one, we needed the extra money; and two, I honestly think it was tough for him to see me pregnant. I was about three months pregnant when I turned 16, so of course a pin could drop and cause a ruckus. My mama often knew what my mouth didn't say, and she's the kind of person who neither you nor your body could lie to. She could notice your breathing from a distance and tell you, "Go take your asthma spray." So with me lacking iron or needing anything wouldn't go unnoticed. One day I sat at the edge of the counter and she started to cook. I didn't ask or complain about any issues, but she started cooking something I'd never seen in the skillet. It was liver. At this point I was just trying to enjoy a moment where things weren't too uncomfortable or sad, so I just waited. Once it was done she fixed me a plate of grits to go with it. I took one bite and thought, "What the hell, this is amazing!" Turns out, back in the day they would give pregnant women liver to help with their battle with iron. Even if you don't care for the liver, the light gravy that comes off is mind-blowing. Serve over rice or hot grits!

1 pound chicken livers, rinsed and trimmed and cut into 3-inch pieces
2 cups whole milk
2 tablespoons olive oil
6 to 8 strips bacon, chopped into bite-sized pieces
2 medium onions, peeled and sliced
4 tablespoons butter
2 tablespoons all-purpose flour
1 cup chicken broth
Salt and pepper

1 Soak the chicken liver in the milk for 1 hour.

2 Using a large skillet over medium heat, heat the olive oil and add the bacon. Cook for 5 minutes, stirring a few times. Add the onions and cook for 10 minutes or until softened.

3 Using a slotted spoon, remove the bacon and onions onto a plate. Leave 2 tablespoons of the bacon grease in the skillet.

4 Heat the grease over medium-high heat and add the chicken liver. Cook for 5 minutes, or until the chicken liver is cooked through, flipping on the other side once. Remove the chicken liver onto a plate.

5 Now, melt 2 tablespoons of the butter with the flour over medium heat. Stir until everything is combined, about 1 minute. Pour in the chicken broth. Season with salt and pepper and whisk until it comes to a gentle boil and the sauce is thickened.

6 Return the chicken liver and bacon with onions back into the pan, stir with the sauce, and let everything heat through, about 1 minute.

CHICKEN NOODLE SOUP

6 SERVINGS

My mama is so good with soups, and I think it was the healer within that always chimed in when she was cooking. Watching my pregnant belly grow, she was hurt for many reasons. She didn't have many words for me, she just had feelings. I would tell her what I felt like eating, but she didn't say much, she just cooked. She cooked whatever I wanted, and now looking back it was all a conversation through food. A loving gesture that she only could express through flavor from the works of her hands. It really was chicken noodle soup for my soul. The warmest redemption a troubled heart could receive. Thank you, Mama; I heard you in every bite.

5 tablespoons olive oil

3 garlic cloves, minced

1 onion, diced

4 celery stalks, minced

4 large carrots, cut in half lengthwise and sliced

Salt

Pepper

5 boneless chicken breasts

Rotisserie chicken or poultry seasoning blend

12 cups water

4 chicken bouillon cubes

2 bay leaves

4 tablespoons fresh parsley

1 (12-ounce) bag egg noodles

1 Heat 3 tablespoons of the olive oil in a stockpot. Add the garlic, onions, celery, and carrots along with a pinch of salt and pepper. Sauté for 8 to 10 minutes, until fragrant and tender. Set aside.

2 Season the chicken with the seasoning blend. In a large skillet, add the remaining 2 tablespoons of the olive oil. Sear and cook chicken for 5 to 7 minutes on each side. Then shred chicken and set aside.

3 Add the 12 cups of water and bouillon cubes to create chicken broth in the pot with the veggies.

4 Once the soup is boiling, reduce heat to low, add the bay leaves and parsley to the pot. Allow the soup to simmer for 15 minutes.

5 Add the chicken to the soup and the egg noodles. Simmer for an additional 15 minutes, or until the noodles are tender.

6 Add more salt and pepper to the soup if needed before serving.

COLLARD GREENS

4 TO 6 SERVINGS

Collards are rich in vitamins, minerals, and fiber. They can help revitalize sore muscles and are said to improve mood, sleep, and memory. They are a good source of iron, which is important for pregnant women, because they help replenish what the baby growing inside of them is pulling so relentlessly. That's why my mama made them for me. Serve alone, with rice, or with a protein.

¼ cup butter

2 teaspoons chopped garlic or 2 garlic cloves, chopped

1 onion, peeled and chopped

1 bell pepper, destemmed, deseeded, and chopped

½ celery stalk, chopped

1 (32-ounce) bag triple-washed collard greens

1 to 2 cups chicken or vegetable stock

Cajun seasoning or seasoned salt

1 teaspoon lime juice (optional)

1 In a large saucepan, melt 2 tablespoons of the butter over medium heat.

2 Add the garlic and sauté for 1 to 2 minutes.

3 Add the trinity (onion, bell pepper, celery) and continue to cook until tender, about 7 minutes.

4 Add the remaining butter and the collards. Sauté until the collards begin to wilt slightly, approximately 10 minutes.

5 Add a cup or two of stock at this stage for more tender greens; simmer for an additional 5 minutes.

6 Begin to season to taste with the Cajun seasoning. Add the lime juice, if using, and remove from heat.

FRENCH FRIES 4 WAYS

4 SERVINGS

My love for french fries grew deeper than a pregnancy craving. They were my go-to whenever I went out, especially once I started reading poetry at the open mic nights. French fries were one of the things my daddy would make for me if I didn't want to eat what was cooked for dinner. Skin on, hot grease in a cast-iron skillet, exuberant bubbles rising up to the edges of the pan. Nothing gets better than that. He would chop up two potatoes in two minutes and fry them up short-order-cook style. Sometimes I felt as if my daddy was a magician. He could cook and build and draw, and it felt as if what he could do was never ending. Because of him, as a kid I preferred fresh fries over store-bought, but, hey, I'd take what I could get as long as they were fried, hot, and the salt was put on immediately after so it could stick. As my daddy would say, "Toy, you gotta put the salt on when it's hot out the grease or it's gonna bounce off." So that's how I like 'em and, no lie, I love soggy fries too! This is a twice-fried method I use and here's a bunch of ways you can make them, all delicious, and all will strike a chord of comfort because that's what fries do. So let it do what it do.

TRADITIONAL FRENCH FRIES

6 russet potatoes (1 to 2 potatoes per person)
Vegetable cooking oil for frying (you want about 4 inches deep)
Salt and pepper to taste or Cajun seasoning

1 Rinse the potatoes under cold water if you're going to keep the skin on. Personally, I love the skin; it gives a home-cooked feel, in my opinion. Otherwise, peel the potatoes.

2 Slice the potatoes into ¼-inch sticks with a large knife, place them in a bowl filled with water, and soak them for an hour.

3 Rinse them with water and pat them dry. This is an important step!

4 Heat the oil to 300°F and fry the fries for 5 to 6 minutes, until they are cooked and still pale. Transfer the par-cooked fries to a large baking sheet lined with paper towels. Fry in batches so you don't overcrowd the pan. Repeat with all remaining fries.

5 Now, increase the heat to 400°F and fry them again for 3 minutes. Then drain them on paper towels again, but this time immediately sprinkle them with salt and pepper and serve.

4 WAYS

1

Spread the fries on a baking sheet and sprinkle with your favorite cheeses. Put under the broiler until the cheese is bubbling and serve piping hot.

2

Serve with roast beef or pot roast with gravy on top!

3

Toss with truffle oil and sautéed garlic, and sprinkle grated Parmesan and parsley on top!

4

Sushi topping: In one of our classes at culinary school, a sushi chef came in to give a demonstration to teach us how to make sushi. On top of making sushi I loved making sushi bowls, so combining a sushi bowl with fries was a win-win! Top the fries with shredded imitation crabmeat (1 cup per serving of fries), drizzle hoisin sauce and sriracha mayo, and top with toasted sesame seeds. I promise it will blow your mind!

PEPPERONI LASAGNA

6 TO 8 SERVINGS

After the baby was born, I got another job to help with small stuff like dia-pers or other things I needed. This time I wasn't cooking and getting paid under the table. It was a legit job, a fresh start. It was a new world for me, trying to reset after such a rough turn of becoming a parent. Even though I wasn't cooking, I got to see food all day and the store had a chef who made weekly specials, and this man's lasagna was the best. Cheesy, saucy, and salty! I discovered in between the layers he put pepperonis along with the meat, and man it was top notch! So when my first birthday as a mother rolled around, and honestly, I wasn't going to mention it because of how the last birthday ended up in Planned Parenthood, my mama walked up and asked what I wanted to eat for my birthday, and without hesitation I told her about the lasagna. She made it seem super simple once I explained it. "So it's just lasagna with pepperoni added?" she asked. I said, "Well yeah, that's it!" She made that for me, and that birthday dish was a taste of what normal was in the midst of the new adult normal I was now living. The 17-year-old me loved it. I think you will too . . .

FOR THE LASAGNA

1 pound ground beef

½ pound sweet Italian sausage

1 medium onion, chopped

2 garlic cloves, minced

1 (15-ounce) can tomato sauce

1 (15-ounce) can crushed tomatoes

2 (6-ounce) cans tomato paste

½ cup water

2 tablespoons sugar

3 teaspoons salt

3 teaspoons Italian seasoning

1½ teaspoons dried basil leaves

¼ teaspoon ground black pepper

¼ cup minced fresh flat-leaf parsley

15 ounces (1¾ cups) whole milk ricotta cheese

2 cups shredded mozzarella cheese

½ cup grated Parmesan

1 large egg

12 lasagna noodles

1 (6-ounce) package pepperoni, sliced

FOR THE ITALIAN CRÈME FRAÎCHE

12 ounces crème fraîche

1 teaspoon Italian seasoning

1 teaspoon chopped garlic

½ teaspoon of salt

TO MAKE THE LASAGNA

1 Preheat the oven to 350°F.

2 Make the meat sauce. Add the beef and sausage to a large skillet over medium-high heat, breaking it apart with a wooden spoon. Add the onion and garlic. Cook until the meat is browned, 6 to

CONTINUES

8 minutes. Drain the fat from the meat. Return the meat to the skillet.

3   Add the tomato sauce, crushed tomatoes, tomato paste, water, sugar, 2 teaspoons of the salt, 2 teaspoons of the Italian seasoning, 1 teaspoon of the basil, and the black pepper. Stir until well combined. Cover and reduce the heat to low. Simmer the sauce for 30 minutes. Stir in 2 tablespoons of the minced parsley.

4   As the sauce cooks, make the ricotta mixture. In a large bowl, add 1 cup of the mozzarella, the ricotta, 1/4 cup of the Parmesan, 2 tablespoons of the parsley, the egg, 1 teaspoon salt, 1 teaspoon Italian seasoning, and 1/2 teaspoon basil. Stir until well incorporated.

5   Cook the pasta al dente, according to the directions on the package.

6   Assemble the lasagna. In a 13-by-9-inch baking dish, add a very thin layer of meat sauce (about 1/4 cup). Layer the pepperoni, 3 lasagna noodles, one-third of the ricotta mixture, and 1½ (level) cups of meat sauce. Repeat the layers twice.

7   Add a final layer of the remaining noodles, meat sauce, 1 cup mozzarella, and 1/4 cup Parmesan.

8   Cover with foil that has been sprayed with nonstick cooking spray. Bake for 45 minutes. Remove the foil. Bake 15 more minutes.

9   Let the lasagna cool for 15 to 20 minutes before cutting.

TO MAKE THE ITALIAN CRÈME FRAÎCHE

1   Mix together the crème fraîche, Italian seasoning, chopped garlic, and salt until well blended. Spoon a hearty tablespoon or two on the plate before placing the lasagna on top.

Emily Taught Me

Through the hands of Emily many things were built
4'11" she stands but her heart's on stilts
A Leo with fiery kickback like a pistol
Smooth like a brush with no bristles
Trials falling down like missiles
Many tears cried
no time for tissue
She's the strongest woman I know
Wisdom from 9 lifetimes
She's invincible
Any child near her palms was molded to know that they count,
they matter
Taught not to accept the world's ability to flatter
Never to trust those with reckless chatter
And when bad things happen, get up and choose the latter
Learning lessons is the only way to become greater
The consequences of walking crooked will teach you to walk straighter
Think twice, never swing first, keep low key in behavior
Stay humble and aligned with the Creator
But air that bitch out if need be
And if anything falls apart you'll always have me.

MAMA

CHAPTER THREE

MAINS

New Orleans food cultures

Creole, as it pertains to food, culture, or people, is influenced by a mix of cultures.

Creole people are generally a blend of African, French, and Spanish, and their foods have flavors from West Africa, France, and Spain. Those blends show up in every single part of the New Orleans experience. The buildings and architecture reflect a heavy Spanish and French influence. In New Orleans, you hear Creole talked about mostly pertaining to the food and the people. The food gives a telltale sign of Creole by the cooking: the proteins (seafood predominates), the seasonings (oregano, basil, thyme, rosemary, or paprika), the textures (smooth and creamier at times), and the techniques (the use of the butter roux or the addition of okra as a thickening agent, from the Africans). Africans were behind the big bang that New Orleans contributed to the food culture. Many of the meals in this book were first cooked by slaves from the rations given to them.

When it comes to Cajuns, it's a lot different than explaining Creole. The Cajun people were the Acadians, French colonists who settled in the Acadia region of Canada. In the 1700s, they were removed by the British and many settled in the fertile bayou lands of southern Louisiana. Their food was from the wild of the land and waters. Now, you may not know this but in order to cook anything "wild" you need to be crafty. By crafty I mean you have to know how to flavor and mask the gamy taste of non-traditional meats. For example, chicken, beef, pork, and fish are what I would call traditional meats: They don't have a "wild" taste and their flavors are easily masked with seasonings and cooking fats. But alligator, squirrel, raccoon, or even frog legs require a little more love in the seasoning depart-

ment. I didn't include turkey among the traditional meats, because in my opinion you have to do more work in terms of herbs, spices, and brining to rid turkey of its gamy taste. But I will say that I think people are so wrapped up in the nostalgia of the holidays, and really only eat turkey once a year, so they don't notice the gamy taste. Even so, turkey has that "I've been running around in the wild" flavor that we label as a "game" taste. It's definitely there. So for those reasons Cajun food tends to have a heavier well-seasoned taste, and that's always a shock to tourists who visit Louisiana. Cajuns do have spicier meals in comparison to Creole. Even if you buy a Cajun or a Creole spice blend, you'll notice that one is spicier than the other.

I am a fan of Cajun foods because of my father. While my mama has a very traditional Creole New Orleanian style of cooking and I love that as well. Some of my fondest memories are attached to Creole dishes. My daddy was an adventurous cook because he worked offshore welding and liked to fish, so he got to know a lot of Cajuns. He'd try different Cajun foods, and he'd sometimes come home with deer sausage, frog legs, and whatnot. And my daddy makes the *best* rabbit stew! As a kid I would ask to try things and I was never afraid. I learned from him, "Don't eat from anyone who doesn't know how to remove glands from an animal, it'll taste *horrible*." Cajun cooking is often summarized as blackened and spicy, but it's a real art form that's not just spice. Cajuns have a real connection with the land and its animals, and the Creoles have a deep connection with the people, cultures, and traditions that makes their food so memorable.

FRIED SHRIMP & ROCAFELLA CREAM

4 TO 6 SERVINGS

This recipe has a story that's tied to my very first pink slip. I was a waitress once, and you guessed right: I wasn't a good one either. I was excellent at talking to guests, but I was bad at getting the orders right. Working after high school felt a lot like school. I couldn't get anything right. I came into work after an off day ready to start my shift and the manager caught me before I clocked in and issued my pink slip that read, "Toya is not cut out to be a waitress." I wasn't mad because I was pretty honest with myself, and I could admit all the times I messed up stuff on my shift. I told my daddy about it and he looked at me and said, "Well it's good you know." Something about that gave me a sliver of hope. I still dealt with some sad moments because of it, because I'm human and of course I thought, "Damn you can't even get that right." It was just another moment that I can look back at and think that it was another closed door pushing me to find the right one. Getting fired didn't stop me from ordering my favorite meal to go. Anytime I had extra money to blow, I'd order it to go! The meal was a fried shrimp dish with a spinach cream over pasta. The fried and creamy combo is outstanding. Here's my version.

FOR THE SHRIMP

Vegetable oil for frying
2 large eggs
1 cup buttermilk or milk
4 tablespoons Cajun seasoning
1½ cups all-purpose flour
1 cup cornmeal
1 teaspoon smoked paprika
**2 pounds prawns or jumbo
    shrimp, peeled and deveined**
Cream sauce, recipe follows

FOR THE SPINACH
CREAM SAUCE

2 tablespoons salted butter
¼ cup chopped onion
1 tablespoon chopped garlic
3 tablespoons cornstarch
3 cups half-and-half
1 teaspoon smoked paprika
**½ teaspoon cracked black
    pepper, more for serving**

1 teaspoon salt, more as needed
**½ teaspoon red pepper flakes
    (optional)**
2 cups fresh spinach

TO MAKE THE SHRIMP

1 Heat ½ inch of oil in a large, heavy-bottomed skillet over medium heat. Line a large plate with a paper towel, set aside.

CONTINUES

2 In a container, whisk together the eggs and buttermilk. Add 2 table-spoons of the Cajun seasoning.

3 In another container, mix together the flour, cornmeal, 2 table-spoons of the Cajun seasoning, and smoked paprika.

4 Add the shrimp to the egg mixture and coat well. A few at a time, add the shrimp to the flour and coat completely. Place on a clean plate while you bread the remaining shrimp.

5 Add the shrimp to the skillet, making sure not to overcrowd the pan. Fry for 4 minutes, or until crispy and golden brown. Drain on a plate lined with paper towels.

TO MAKE THE SPINACH CREAM SAUCE

1 Over medium heat, melt the butter and sauté the onions and garlic until tender and fragrant, about 5 minutes.

2 Whisk the cornstarch into the half-and-half, then immediately add it to the pan with sautéed onions and garlic.

3 Add the paprika, pepper, salt, and red pepper flakes, if using. Whisk until blended and simmer until it thickens, 5 to 8 minutes.

4 Once it has thickened up, add the spinach and extra salt if needed.

5 Spoon the sauce on the plate and pile up the shrimp, sprinkle with extra pepper, and serve.

The Trinity

The "holy trinity," yes, the father, son, and holy spirit of the food world is made up of onions, celery, and bell peppers. It's the basic blend of chopped seasoning that we put into the majority of our meals in New Orleans. The French have a similar blend called mirepoix, which is made up of onions, celery, and carrots. The traditional mirepoix is two parts onions, one part carrots, and one part celery, whereas the holy trinity is typically two parts onions, one part green bell pepper, and one part celery. The trinity was another baby birthed from the blending of the African, French, and Spanish cultures among the early settlers in New Orleans, known as Creole. As a child, I'd see my mama adding a green liquid to all of her meals and I never questioned it. Well, in culinary school we went over the mirepoix and examined its close relation to the trinity, and then it dawned on me! My mama used the trinity in everything! The ingredients were put in a food processor, blended into a liquid, and added to the pot. It was a habit she picked up from cooking things the way her father wanted, because he didn't want to see chopped seasoning in his meals.

Now you can find this seasoning frozen or fresh in just about every store! I think the blended way my mama did it is perfect for those who don't like chopped seasoning. But for those who don't mind it chopped, a great deal more flavor can be gotten out of these simple ingredients by following some simple techniques. First you sauté half of them to bring out the caramelization. You just cook them slowly until they soften; I like to call that "sweating." Then you mix the caramelized half with the rest of the raw ingredients. The combination of caramelized and raw gives a layering of flavors. And that's what it's all about. The flavor.

JAMBALAYA

8 TO 10 SERVINGS

I can hear Mrs. Valbuena yelling down the hallway, "Slow down, mamacita; you have a baby in your belly!" I was always running late to Spanish class, because the class before Spanish was on the opposite side of the school. So in my 10th grade mind, I needed to run. So funny that I always ran to a class I was always failing, because I was horrible at retaining Spanish . . . or was it "pregnancy brain" that made me forget? I know one thing: Mrs. Pilar Valbuena cared for me. She even threw me a baby shower in class. Yes, in Spanish class I had a baby shower. Well after the baby was born, deep into senior year, I had Spanish again. And again, I was failing. Mrs. Valbuena called me to the desk to tell me, "Mamacita, you are failing, and you need this class to graduate." She suggested I take makeup quizzes, and I, in a quick response, replied, "Oh, you know Imma fail that, what about extra credit projects?" She agreed. I made paella, Spanish rice, and a series of elaborate piñatas. I swear I can make a mean piñata and set of maracas too. I always say my creativity helped me graduate high school. That was my first time making paella, and while making it I noticed heavy similarities to a dish my mama made: jambalaya. I was amazed. Jambalaya is a rice dish birthed in Louisiana when the Spanish made a modified version of paella using tomatoes instead of saffron, and this is the version that we call Creole jambalaya, or red jambalaya. It has a smooth taste because of the tomato flavor. The same dish was cooked by the Cajuns, which was spicier, and brown because of the spices, smoked meats, and deeply caramelized vegetables. Cajun, or brown, jambalaya has a smoky boldness.

Although paella is a big influencer of jambalaya, it isn't the only influence. A few African rice and meat–based dishes come to mind, like jollof, waakye, and cabidela. Jambalaya is also another one of those meals in the food culture of New Orleans that is known for its affordability to make and its ability to stretch. That alone makes me throw the African hat in the ring for being one of the influences of jambalaya. If any of the native Spanish or Africans craved any rice dish from home, they had to use what was available to them in Louisiana. Take your cues from them to make jambalaya that's specific to where you live, and that caters to the people who come to your table. In our home growing up, we always had red jambalaya because a great deal of my mama's cooking techniques leaned toward a Creole style of cooking and flavoring. Now, as an adult, I enjoy the smokiness of the brown as well. But if my mama's at the table, it's going to be red.

3 tablespoons vegetable oil

2 pounds boneless chicken
     breast, chopped or cubed

3 to 4 tablespoons Cajun
     seasoning, more to taste

2 pounds smoked sausage

2 pounds medium shrimp,
     peeled and deveined

3½ cups chopped yellow onions

1½ cups chopped green bell
     peppers

1½ cups chopped celery

8¼ cups chicken stock

2 tablespoons tomato paste

2 (14-ounce) cans diced
     tomatoes

1 heaping tablespoon chopped
     garlic

7 cups uncooked Ben's Original
     rice (parboiled)

1 bay leaf

2 cups chopped green onions

1 In a large pot, add the oil and bring to a medium heat.

2 Lightly season the chicken with the Cajun seasoning. Brown the chicken and set aside. In the same pot, without changing the oil, sauté the sausage for 8 minutes. (This will leave more fat in the bottom of the pot. You want all the juices from all the meats to be at the bottom of the pot.) Once the sausage is nice and sticky, remove and set aside. Last, sauté the shrimp in the fat for 5 minutes, and then set aside. This will lock all the flavor at the bottom of the pot!

3 Now, add the trinity mixture and green onions to the pot and begin to sauté for 8 minutes. Once softened, add the stock, paste, tomatoes, and garlic and bring to a boil.

4 Immediately after the boiling point is reached, add the rice, chicken, sausage, and bay leaf.

5 Season with the Cajun seasoning to taste.

6 Reduce the heat to a simmer and cook for 25 minutes, stirring occasionally. Add the shrimp for the last 7 minutes of cooking.

7 Once the 7 minutes are up, remove from the heat. If the rice is tender, serve immediately. But if you feel the rice is a little too firm, stir it around and put the lid on until it's tender. Trust me, the heat from the pot will finish the job.

SMOTHERED CHICKEN

4 TO 6 SERVINGS

I can smell it like it was yesterday, walking into the house and smelling "that smell," which I now know is the smell of the roux. Going straight to the kitchen counter, super-hot after walking home from the bus stop with my rapidly growing belly, hoping that the gravy I smell has delicious corn to go with it. As always, my mama made the best damn smothered chicken, or as I called it "gravy, rice, and corn." This is one meal I will never get tired of, nothing but warm memories attached to it. Man, don't talk about the corn sitting in the gravy, oh my gawd. It's a dream come true.

4 to 6 boneless chicken breasts or thighs

Cajun seasoning or seasoned salt

1 cup plus 2 tablespoons canola or vegetable oil

1 cup flour

6 to 8 cups chicken stock

1 onion, chopped

1 bell pepper, chopped

1 celery stalk, chopped

2 tablespoons chopped garlic

1 bunch of parsley, chopped

Cooked rice for serving

1 Season the chicken with Cajun seasoning, generously.

2 Add 2 tablespoons of the oil to a large saucepan or pot. Heat at medium heat and brown the chicken on both sides. (This locks in the flavor and seasoning into the chicken.) Remove the chicken from the pan and set aside.

3 To make the roux: Over medium heat, add 1 cup of the oil to the pan. Add the flour to the oil and whisk it around; it will turn tan almost immediately because of the bits from the chicken and the seasoning and that's a good thing—don't worry!

4 Stir for a few minutes at medium-low heat to achieve a deep tan color. Remove from heat.

5 Add the stock. Whisk at medium heat until the stock is well blended with the roux. Then return to heat.

6 Add the chopped vegetables (the trinity: onion, pepper, celery), parsley, and garlic.

7 Season to taste with Cajun seasoning.

8 Add the chicken breasts to the pan and allow them to simmer for 15 to 20 minutes. Remember, the chicken isn't cooked all the way yet. It will finish cooking in the gravy. If you want to use thighs or any other part, season *really* well, then let them cook in the gravy for 45 minutes to 1 hour.

9 Once the chicken is cooked through, adjust the seasoning again because the chicken releases water when you cook it, so it may water down the seasoning level.

10 Serve over cooked rice.

Roux

I'm not saying you have to be an amazing cook, you at least need to know how to smother something.

Roux is the boogeyman of many kitchens. Over the years I've heard countless people embrace cooking in many different areas, but stay clear out of the path of all things roux related. I'm sure someone's thinking, "Toya, you don't get it. I've tried!" But before you declare it "impossible," there's a few things that you need to know. First, let's break down the roux-making process. There's one thing that everyone leaves out, and that's fear. Fear should be the first thing addressed, because we've all heard stories about the burned roux and how it ruined the gumbo, gravy, or even the cook's reputation. How do we stop the fear? Simple. Fear can be silenced with facts and strategy.

It's a fact that a roux is one part fat to one part flour, basically. However much fat you use, the equal amount of flour will be needed. This costs well under $1 to make. Isn't it a tinge less intimidating to know that making a roux is so cheap *and* it only takes two ingredients?

Next up is strategy. The strategy is based on "kitchen comfort," and kitchen comfort is based on your confidence level. So the person teaching you how to make a roux should use a technique that's more foolproof instead of the exact method they use, which is wrapped around their level of comfort.

A good strategy is all wrapped around order. Order is like a seat belt while cooking. Have the tools and ingredients laid out, and read the recipe three times. Reading the recipe three times is a tactic I use myself when encountering a recipe for the first time. By the third time you've read it, you can begin to feel the steps happening in your mind. You can begin to see it clearly, and you haven't even begun the cooking process.

There's two types of roux that we use in our recipes: one type uses butter; the other type uses lard or oil.

The butter roux is the beginning of a béchamel, bisque, étouffée base, or any creamy, rich gravy or soup. The flavor profile for this roux has a more delicate feel. White gravy for biscuits is a perfect example. It's gotta be so smooth.

The lard or oil roux is for a bold flavor profile like poultry gravy, game, red gravy, and gumbo.

The butter roux has three shades: blonde, light khaki, and peanut butter. It also has a nutty essence.

A butter roux has a good deal of safety attached to it. Let's take a blonde roux for example. For the blonde roux, you aren't changing colors, you're adding butter to the pan, letting it melt, and *immediately* after you're adding the flour, whisking until well blended, then adding liquids. It's pretty stress free, and it's more of a dump-and-stir kind of thing. The étouffée roux isn't too scary because it gets to a peanut butter color a lot faster than a lard- or oil-based roux. Butter burns past a certain point, so it stops at the peanut butter color.

The lard or oil roux has a wider range of colors because the fat used has the ability to get really hot without burning, and that cooks the flour to create the color changes you see happening.

The lard or oil roux starts blonde and gradually moves from shade to shade until it hits a chocolate color. Each color of the lard or oil roux has a purpose. For example, a turkey gravy is light khaki but close to the nut brown, and it's only lighter because typically this roux is made from the turkey drippings and fat. But, yes, you can use fat from other animals! The gravy typically has bits from the turkey and seasonings that can burn quickly during the cooking of the roux, so it's best to stop it early so the bits don't burn, which will result in the gravy tasting as if the roux was burned. Peanut butter–colored roux is for smothered chicken, pork chops, or a beef gravy. Deep peanut butter or light chocolate color is a good spot for a beginner's gumbo, and a chocolate color is for the cooking vets or the brave.

The smell of the lard or oil roux can be a major contributor to the fear of making the roux. Our minds, when under pressure, will pick up on the "bitter" smell that comes from the darker hues of roux and misread it for "burned."

Do not declare the roux is burned until you see black bits. You can avoid the burn scares by firmly committing to a "stirring style." I suggest adopting one of these two styles of stirring the roux:

STYLE 1: Outer, outer, inner, inner: Stir the outer rim twice and then the center twice, always covering the entire pan to make sure that one part isn't cooking faster than the other.

CONTINUES

STYLE 2: Whisk every part of the pan in no uniform fashion inside or outside, just keep the roux moving.

Both styles have one thing in common: keeping the roux moving at all times! It's like babysitting a baby that just started crawling—you can't shift focus. Some of your protection comes from the temperatures of the burner and the roux itself. I recommend starting the roux at a medium heat and changing it to low once it gets to a peanut butter color, so you can take your time graduating from color to color.

My opinion as an instructor is for you to stop at a peanut butter color for your first gumbo, because there are so many other factors that you have to consider past that point. For a first time, they can be overwhelming. We all can collectively admit that the first of anything is scary, and that the minutes may seem to stretch to hours. The room always seems hotter on those days, and it also always seems to be the exact day everyone needs to call you for something. So you need to give yourself space to grow upward. After all, no one leaves the womb knowing how to make a roux, so the lighter color will help you grow confident enough to realize, "Hey, *I can do this!*"

Now, as a native of New Orleans, my opinion of roux is much different. As a local, you *do not* want to offer a gumbo lacking that deep melanin color to a native, nor do you want to post pictures of it on the internet without a disclaimer. Don't add stuff you'd put in a stew and slap the word "authentic" on it. Just call whatever you're making "soup," because it's not an authentic gumbo.

All of this information can be combed through a few times and can help you on your smothering journey, leaving you knowledgeable and "kitchen confident."

SEAFOOD GUMBO

10 SERVINGS

You can't talk about gumbo without mentioning how it came about. The word gumbo comes from ki ngombo, *which is the West African word for "okra." West Africans used okra as a thickener for the original gumbo, because okra is mucilaginous—it contains a slimy substance. Yes, the very first gumbo was made from okra by the Africans. It was like a stew, and they made it using the rations and scraps they were given. So many different thickening agents have been used to make gumbo throughout history, and it leads me to believe that the reason for the changes may have been more out of necessity than flavor. First came the okra for gumbo, then came filé gumbo. We can thank the Native Americans for filé. Filé is an herbal powder made from the dried and ground leaves of the sassafras tree (Sassafras albidum). It's a thickening agent added at the end of cooking, and it has an earthy flavor. The introduction of the roux happened later from taking the French roux technique used for their creamy soups. Instead of using butter, the Africans substituted animal fat. This is the type of fat used most today. In New Orleans, our gumbo tastes different from the gumbo you will get anywhere else. Typically when you go to someone's house in New Orleans you'll be served a seafood gumbo. Rarely will you go to someone's house and be served an okra or filé gumbo as the main dish, because those are considered a specialty or acquired taste gumbo. We as New Orleanians take gumbo seriously, and we take time to build the flavor because we know that everything contributes to the flavor, taking it from "This is good" to "Damn, you made this?!" That's where everyone wants to be, on the pleasant side of surprise.*

1 cup oil

1 cup flour

2 small onions, chopped finely

1 celery stalk, chopped finely

1 bell pepper, chopped finely

2 (16-ounce) boxes chicken stock

2 (16-ounce) boxes chicken broth

6 garlic cloves, minced

1 (16-ounce) package sausage links, sliced horizontally

4 hot sausage patties or ground hot sausage (removed from its casing)

2 boneless chicken breasts, cut in mini cubes or shredded

1 pound fresh shrimp, peeled and deveined

2 pounds crawfish with fat

1 pound gumbo crabs or crab legs

1 teaspoon crab, shrimp, and crawfish boil (liquid concentrate)

Cajun seasoning or seasoning salt

Cooked rice for serving

CONTINUES

1 Prepare your roux by heating the oil over medium-high heat in a large skillet. Once the oil is hot, you will begin to see ripples at the bottom of the pan.

2 Add the flour and whisk until a deep chocolate color.

3 Add the onions, celery, and bell pepper to the roux (the trinity). Mix quickly and move to the next step immediately.

4 Add the two boxes of chicken stock and two boxes of the broth.

5 Whisk the roux, trinity, and liquid thoroughly together.

6 Add the garlic. Allow the liquid to simmer thoroughly over medium-low heat for 15 minutes.

7 Add all the sausage and let it cook for 15 minutes. Add the chicken and let it cook for 20 minutes.

8 Add all the seafood and the crab, shrimp, and crawfish boil liquid. Don't worry, the shrimp and gumbo crabs will cook extremely fast (5 minutes).

9 Skim the fat from the top.

10 Season to taste with Cajun seasoning.

11 Remove from the heat.

12 Serve with rice.

TIP: In our family, we have seafood allergies so we have to be careful. There's one heavy suggestion I carry when it comes to seafood gumbo: Always remove about 6 cups of gumbo before you add the seafood, and allow those 6 cups to be chicken and sausage gumbo only. It's an easy extra step to accommodate someone who has a seafood allergy or dietary restriction.

STOVE-TOP SEAFOOD BOIL

6 SERVINGS

Seafood boils are something we look forward to each year. You get an invite to a gathering and you pray it's a boil, that's how good it is. It's also one of the easiest things to do when you're feeding a group because it's basically a one-pot meal. Plus it has a super easy serving style and cleanup. Boils are normally served on a personal-sized tray. Or you can put each portion in a small foil pan, because a regular plate wouldn't allow for a generous portion that says, "We're glad you came." Either way allows room for a mess but keeps it contained to the direct area of the person eating, and once they've peeled the shrimp, crabs, and eaten everything else they can simply throw the entire tray away.

2 (3-ounce) packages "boil in a bag": crab, shrimp, and crawfish boil seasoning mix or homemade blend (see page 85)

2 sweet onions, peeled and quartered

2 bundles of green onion

3 celery stalks, cut into chunks (size doesn't matter; it's for flavoring the water)

1 whole lemon, cut in half

1 whole orange, cut in half

2 garlic bulbs

6 new potatoes cut into halves

2 (13-ounce) sausage links, cut into chunks (Cajun smoked sausage or andouille preferred)

8 mini ears frozen corn, defrosted (fresh will take too long to cook with this method)

2 sticks (1 cup) unsalted butter

3 pounds raw shrimp, cleaned (see Tips)

2 pounds crab, cleaned (see Tips; cleaning requires 2 cups salt)

1 Fill an extra large stockpot with water and bring to a boil. Add the seasoning (homemade or store-bought), sweet and green onions, celery, lemon, orange, and garlic to the pot. Bring to a boil.

2 When the water is simmering, carefully add the potatoes, sausage, and corn. Boil until almost fork tender, about 10 minutes. You want the potatoes to still be a little bit firm, as they will remain in the liquid while everything else is cooking and soaking.

3 Add the butter and cleaned shrimp and crabs to the boiling liquid, then immediately cover the pan and remove from heat. Don't worry, the liquid is *so* hot that the seafood will cook while it's

CONTINUES

resting in the pot. At this point your focus is the soaking so the flavor can make it past the shells or the seafood. That's where the magic happens.

4   After 15 minutes of soaking, you can begin to set up the serving trays and paper towels.

TIPS: Shrimp for boils have to be cleaned, but you want to keep the head and shell on. All of that will contribute to the flavor. Besides, removing the head and shell will make the shrimp cook so fast that they will become overdone and they won't soak up the flavor of the broth. We peel the shrimp when it's time to eat. To clean them, soak the raw shrimp in cold water for 10 minutes, then rinse them at least three times or until the water is clear.

Live crabs have to be cleaned a specific way, using a method called purging. Fill up one side of the sink with cold water and 2 cups salt. Add the live crabs to the salty water. Let them sit for 20 minutes. During this soaking time the crabs will release dirt. When the 20 minutes are up, rinse the crabs and they'll be ready to add to the pot when it's time.

HOMEMADE SEAFOOD BOIL SEASONING

1 STOVE-TOP BOIL

In New Orleans, you can find seafood boil seasoning on the shelves. It's becoming more popular to do seafood boils, so it may not be hard to find these products in your local grocery stores. If you can't find it and don't want to wait for it to come in the mail, make your own! Personalize it as well! Remember, the flavor has to be strong in the water in order for it to flavor everything in the pot properly. It might be a little nerve racking for someone who has never seen it made because it will seem like it's going to be too salty. But it isn't. In fact, you might taste the boil broth and think, "Hmmm, maybe a little more salt." A scared cook can't bring big flavor.

¾ cup whole mustard seeds

¾ cup whole coriander seeds

½ cup coarse sea salt

¼ cup celery seeds

¼ cup marjoram

¼ cup dill seeds

2 tablespoons sugar

1 tablespoon whole allspice seeds

1 tablespoon ground red pepper

1 teaspoon whole cloves

2 medium bay leaves, crushed

Add all the spices together and mix well. Store in an airtight jar or container.

TIP: This makes enough for one boil and will last premade for 3 to 6 months.

BBQ SHRIMP

2 TO 4 SERVINGS

There's one thing about us New Orleanians—we don't mind getting our hands dirty for a meal. This one ain't for the faint of heart. Messy shells, shrimp heads, and dippings dripping from palm to wrist. I remember when I first had it. In New Orleans, you can find guys in different parts of the city selling shrimp they caught earlier that day. They'd be on the side of the road and sell their shrimp from a large cooler. Of course you'd only go to the guys you were familiar with, and that's what my mama did. She'd get about 4 pounds of shrimp and make BBQ shrimp. She'd serve it with bread ripped into pieces that you'd dip in the sauce. It's a sauce that says BBQ but it's not a BBQ sauce. It's more like if you had a BBQ sauce for shrimp in New Orleans, this is what it would taste like. And I'm telling you, it's a damn good meal. I never pass this up, that's how good it is! It's the best appetizer for a group. Just imagine: delicious, buttery, fragrant seafood, great conversation and laughs, and hot French bread. Good times and good memories.

½ cup (1 stick) butter

½ onion, peeled and chopped

6 garlic cloves, minced (about 2 tablespoons)

2 tablespoons Cajun seasoning, more if needed

4 tablespoons Worcestershire sauce

1 tablespoon hot sauce

Juice from ½ lemon (about 2 tablespoons)

¼ cup white wine

1 cup chicken broth

1 pound jumbo shrimp, shell on

2 tablespoons freshly chopped parsley

Hot French bread

1 Preheat a cast-iron skillet over medium heat.

2 Melt 1 tablespoon of the butter in the pan, then add the onion and garlic. Sauté for 5 minutes, or until the vegetables are translucent and slightly browned.

3 Add the Cajun seasoning and stir to coat.

4 Add the Worcestershire sauce and hot sauce and stir to combine.

5 Add the lemon juice, remaining butter, wine, and broth and simmer for 3 to 4 minutes, to allow it to reduce a little.

6 Add the shrimp and parsley, tossing them in the onion mixture, and cooking and flipping as needed until the shells become pink and the shrimp is cooked through on both sides, about 5 minutes total cook time.

7 Remove from the heat and cover. The steam will keep it hot, and also the steam helps you make sure they're fully cooked in the center. I know that, typically, shrimp cook and get rubbery quickly but these are larger than normal and the shell is on, so it takes a little longer to cook.

8 Serve with extra Cajun seasoning and hot French bread to dip in the cooking liquid.

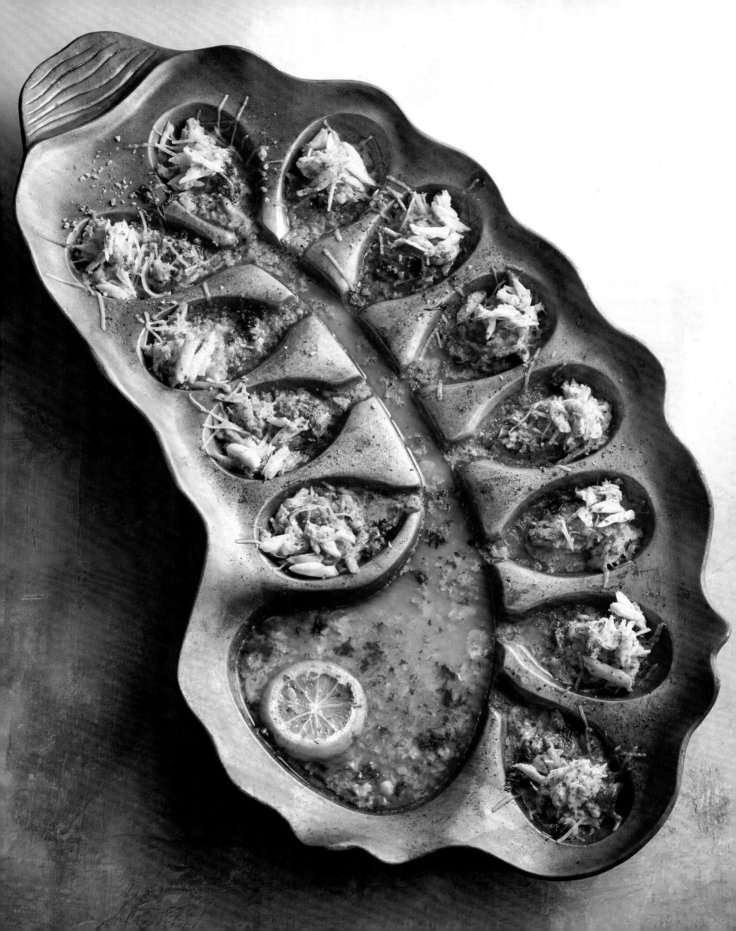

CHARGRILLED OYSTERS WITH BLUE CRABMEAT

6 SERVINGS

I ate my first raw oyster in a parking lot, as part of a presentation during a public speaking class. Before that I only ate them deep fried. One of my classmates was what you'd call a true Cajun. He worked on the water doing all things fishing related. The seafood that comes from the waterways near us is a gold mine for many fishermen. It's their lifeline. For his presentation, my classmate had everyone come out to the parking lot. He told us about the business, and what his days and seasons were like, both the pros and the cons. At the end, he pulled out a bag of oysters from the trunk of his car and said, "This is how you shuck an oyster." He held out the shucked oyster, looked around, and hesitated. Eating a fresh oyster out of a car trunk, from a guy in class who doesn't like to talk to anyone, was beyond everyone's comfort zone. Well, most everyone. As soon as he asked if someone wanted to try it, my hand went up. It was fresh and delicious, and I haven't turned back since. After that I decided to try oysters any way I could find them. My favorite is chargrilled with hot butter, cheese, and crabmeat! You can mix it up any way you want. You can do a large batch of them on the grill, or you can make a small one indoors in the oven. Either way you'll fall in love.

2 dozen oysters in a shell
¼ cup butter, softened
1 tablespoon minced garlic
4 ounces lump blue crabmeat
Cajun seasoning
4 ounces shredded Parmesan cheese
Parsley for garnish

1 If you're using the grill, fire it up! Or, if you prefer to use an oven, preheat it to 400°F and line a sheet pan with foil and set it to the side. Assembly of the oysters won't take long at all, and neither will the cooking, so it's best to have everything prepped and ready in order to make the transition easier.

2 Next we're going to make a quick compound butter. Mix together the softened butter and garlic. Set aside.

3 Now it's time to shuck the oysters. Put one oyster shell in your palm, holding it as flat as possible because you want to preserve as much salty liquid as you can.

4 While holding the shell with one hand, use the oyster or clam knife and gently run it along the crease of the shell; we're looking for a natural groove that would be a good place to jimmy it open, like a dip in the crease. Once you find a spot, gently twist the knife in the

CONTINUES

crease to pop it open. Again, don't do it too swiftly, always keeping that salty liquid in the shell as much as possible.

5 Once it's cracked, don't open it all the way just yet. Still holding the shell firmly, you're going to slide the knife against the inner roof of the shell because the oyster is still attached. You'll know you've gotten it completely off when you feel the shell release. Congratulations! You did it!

6 Now that you've gotten a groove, get them all lined up, begin to spoon on ½ teaspoon of butter (½ teaspoon or a little less depending on the size of the oyster or how generous you want to be with the crab), sprinkle a little Cajun seasoning and cheese, and top with a little parsley. Repeat until they're all prepped. The crab is just like crawfish tails—they have to be steamed in order to remove the meat from the shell, so there's no additional cooking needed.

7 Either grill or bake them until the cheese is melted; they will cook super quickly so get ready to use tongs to pick them up as soon as they're ready! Serve and have fun!

SMOTHERED OKRA & SHRIMP

4 SERVINGS

Smothered okra and shrimp is something of a mystery. You've gotta know the family secrets before you try to take a stab at cooking it. But honey, if it's done right, you can pull out the Captain Morgan stance of victory. My smothered okra and shrimp has a different feel than other versions because of the pork fat and bacon. I got the best compliment from my mama after she got a plate. She said, "The flavor was off the chart. It was very good and a different mission accomplished!" It made me tear up, so I took a screenshot of the text and checked this recipe off as a winner. Normally I'd say that you could maybe use frozen veggies or shrimp, but in this case it's a no-no. It's a temperamental dish, so you have to take time to understand the technique for making it. With practice it becomes easier. Let's jump in!

1 large pack of applewood bacon

1 onion, diced

1 bell pepper, diced

2 heaping tablespoons chopped garlic

2 tablespoons oil

3 cups chopped fresh okra

1 teaspoon white vinegar

2 tablespoons tomato paste

½ cup chicken stock

1 can diced tomatoes, drained

2 to 3 tablespoons Cajun seasoning

1 pound medium-to-large fresh shrimp, peeled and deveined

½ teaspoon crab, shrimp, and crawfish boil (liquid concentrate)

Hot rice

1   Cook the bacon as the package directs in a large skillet over medium-high heat. Save the fat, leaving it in the pan and putting the bacon to the side.

2   Over medium-high heat, sauté the onions, bell pepper, and garlic in the leftover bacon fat until caramelized (about 5 minutes). When done, set the pan aside.

3   Add the oil in a different large skillet, add the okra along with the white vinegar, and gently fold the okra every 40 seconds or so. We're doing this to remove the slime; the heat and vinegar breaks it down. Don't stir the okra—fold it because if you stir, it can smash up the okra more than it needs to be.

4   You'll begin to notice the slime decreasing. Once it's gone, add the okra to the pan with the onion mixture. Add the tomato paste into a measuring cup with the stock and whisk them together. Then add the stock mixture and the diced tomatoes to the okra and veggies. Add the Cajun seasoning.

5   Mix well but still not aggressively. Lower the heat and cover the skillet with the lid, leaving a small crack.

6   Cook for 20 minutes, or until the liquid reduces.

7   Add in the shrimp with the crab, shrimp, and crawfish boil liquid and cook for 5 to 7 minutes.

8   Serve with hot rice and arrange the bacon for each serving.

Fish Plates, Card Games, and Rent Parties: "Get Ya Money Up"

Growing up, good food was a part of everything. Happy moments like weddings or a baby shower, sad moments like a repast for a funeral, and even moments of financial need. If you needed funds of any kind for any reason, you would put a call out to the community for help by throwing a rent party, hosting card games, or hosting a fish fry. The rent party was thrown in order to raise enough money to contribute to the host's rent by paying what you could at the door. For the card games, you paid per table (game). That small fee went to the person hosting the card game. Each player put up whatever the amount was in hopes of winning the pot.

Now the fish fry is something that hasn't phased out. They're being called suppers these days, and anyone can do them. Suppers are a full dinner with a protein, two sides, cake, and a drink, all for one good price. Churches do them to raise money for their ministries. Sometimes a person holds a supper to jump start a new entrepreneurial path! One of my good culinary friends, Chef Natasha Butler (a New Orleans native), did just that.

So these suppers, whether it's fish or chicken plates, are inspiring to me. They demonstrate the good things that can happen if we call out to our community for help, and how the community will show up to help, proving that it not only takes a village, but that the black community *is* one. The thing is that you can't just come to make a withdrawal, you have to make a deposit in some way. The same people hosting the suppers are the same ones feeding people randomly or lending a helping hand to those in need. New Orleans is definitely a city that still has a village mentality. We don't mind helping each other because we know to help someone else is to help ourselves.

FRIED FISH

4 cups buttermilk

¼ cup hot sauce (any brand will do)

1½ pounds boneless, small-to-medium pieces of catfish

1¾ cups white or yellow cornmeal

¼ cup flour

2 teaspoons lemon pepper

1 tablespoon smoked paprika

3 tablespoons Cajun seasoning

Oil for frying

1 Add the buttermilk and hot sauce to a bowl, and whisk well.

2 Add the fish to the buttermilk mixture, cover, and allow it to marinate for 4 hours.

3 Mix all the dry ingredients together.

4 Remove the catfish from the bowl and discard the marinade.

5 Heat the oil over medium-high heat until you see ripples form on the bottom of the large pan, or sprinkle a pinch of the flour mixture in the hot oil. If it sizzles quickly, it is ready for frying.

6 Cover the fish in the seasoned flour on all sides.

7 Fry until the fish is golden and crispy, 5 minutes on each side. Repeat the process until all pieces are fried.

8 Allow the fish to drain on paper towels. Enjoy while hot.

FRIED CHICKEN

4 TO 6 SERVINGS

Fried chicken has to be number two in line after gumbo when it comes to meals that make you terrified. I've seen some great home cooks flinch over frying chicken. Here's my suggestion: get a meat thermometer. Meat thermometers will have a "chicken" setting; otherwise cook until the temperature is 165°F. Use the thermometer to follow the temperature of the chicken as it cooks, and let me tell you, you'll have perfect chicken each time. Cook that chicken and throw it on a plate with some red beans and rice.

8 pieces of chicken
4 cups buttermilk
3 tablespoons minced garlic
2 tablespoons coarse salt
Vegetable oil for frying
2 cups self-rising flour
1 cup cornstarch
2 tablespoons smoked paprika
3 tablespoons Cajun seasoning

1 In a container, add the chicken, buttermilk, garlic, and salt and seal the container. Marinade overnight.

2 Heat 1 inch of vegetable oil in a large, deep skillet (or in a deep fryer) over medium-high heat. The oil is ready when you see ripples at the bottom of the pan or if a pinch of flour sizzles when you drop it in the oil.

3 Mix the flour, cornstarch, and spices in a shallow bowl. Remove one piece of chicken from the buttermilk, shake off the excess buttermilk, and roll it in the flour mixture. Shake off the excess flour and lay on a plate. Repeat the process until all the pieces of chicken are double coated. Place the chicken into the hot oil and fry, turning occasionally, until golden brown and cooked through, about 15 minutes (adjust the heat as needed). Drain on paper towels.

RAVIOLI

3 SERVINGS

Growing up, canned ravioli was like a reward to a kid like me, who got food from scratch every day of the week. Every kid I knew with parents who cooked all the time, like mine did, wanted good ole processed foods. After all, you've gotta realize that's what we saw advertised on TV, so we felt left out. There was something good about a can of ravioli to a teenager after school—it meant we had an option for something other than leftovers. That can was power of choice back then. Here's a lighter version that will comfort you just the same.

3 tablespoons olive oil
1 tablespoon chopped garlic
1 small white onion, chopped
2 pints cherry tomatoes, sliced
    in half
2 basil leaves
½ teaspoon sugar
Salt and cracked pepper
1 (16-ounce) package ravioli

1 Put a large pot of water on the stove to boil.

2 In a large skillet over medium heat, add the olive oil and sauté the garlic and onions for 5 minutes until they're fragrant and slightly caramelized.

3 Add the tomatoes, basil, and sugar and sauté for about 7 minutes, until they begin to break down to form a thin but chunky sauce. Salt and pepper to taste.

4 Meanwhile, cook the ravioli as the package directs. When the ravioli is ready, serve with the tomato sauce.

BAKED MAC & CHEESE

6 TO 8 SERVINGS

This is the type of baked mac and cheese that you bring to show off your skills. It has this richness and full-body flavor that's unmatched. When I created this recipe, I thought of luxurious comfort food. It had to be creamy, it had to feel like rich cream and noodles. It had to be good. This is exactly it.

1 (16-ounce) package of large
    elbow noodles
½ cup (1 stick) butter
3 cups shredded Cheddar
2 cups shredded pepper Jack
3 cups milk
4 ounces whipped cream cheese
4 tablespoons sour cream
1 teaspoon chopped garlic
Salt and cracked pepper to taste

1   Preheat the oven to 400°F.

2   Boil the noodles as the package directs. Drain and immediately return them to the pot.

3   Add the butter and stir until it's fully melted.

4   Add 2 cups of the Cheddar, putting 1 cup to the side for the topping before it goes into the oven. Stir until almost all melted, then add the pepper Jack, milk, sour cream, cream cheese, and garlic and mix well.

5   Salt and pepper to taste. Pour everything into a 2-quart baking dish or 9-by-13-inch pan. Top with the remaining cheese and cracked pepper and bake until the cheese is bubbly and melted, 20 to 25 minutes.

6   Let it cool and set for 15 minutes before serving.

YAKAMEIN

10 SERVINGS

This dish has been floating through our entire lives as locals in New Orleans. It comes directly from the Chinese immigrants who lived in a part of New Orleans that used to be called Chinatown. The dish became super popular, and it actually became one of the things that you'd consume to soothe a hangover. All over the city people started re-creating this delicious dish that the Chinese gifted to the New Orleans food world.

1 (2½-to 3-pound) boneless chuck or eye of round roast
8 to 9 cups water
3 tablespoons beef bouillon
2 teaspoons Cajun seasoning
½ to ⅔ cup soy sauce, more to taste
1 tablespoon sriracha ketchup, more for topping if you like
1 tablespoon Worcestershire sauce
1 (1-pound) package of spaghetti, cooked according to package directions
1 bunch scallions, trimmed and sliced
5 hard-boiled eggs, cut in half
Hot sauce (optional)

1 Place the beef in a large stockpot. Cover with the water and bouillon, and then add the Cajun seasoning. Place over medium-high heat, bring to a simmer, then reduce the heat to low and simmer for 3 to 4 hours, until the beef is tender. Remove the beef to a large bowl and allow the beef and stock to cool for 20 to 30 minutes.

2 Shred or chop the cooled beef, removing and discarding any large chunks of fat. Skim off the fat from the top of the stock. Add the soy sauce, ketchup, Worcestershire sauce, and hot sauce to the stock, tasting as you go and adjusting the seasonings if needed. When you're ready to serve, reheat the skimmed stock over medium heat until simmering.

3 To serve, divide the spaghetti and meat among 10 bowls. Top each with scallions and half an egg, and ladle some stock over the top. Serve with hot sauce or ketchup.

BBQ SALMON

4 SERVINGS

This BBQ salmon plate was from the menu at the club that held open mic nights hosted by poet and educator Frederick "Wood" Delahoussaye and spoken word artist S.M.U.T. The owner of the venue, Joe, had both an amazing menu and a big heart. He allowed me to host benefit concerts for free there. I planned and hosted a series of benefit concerts called T. Church's Party With A Purpose to give back to various groups and causes in the city. I had a vision to give back, and other creatives gave their time for free, just as I did. Singers, rappers, DJs, and poets spread their wings on that stage and I'm forever grateful. The city showed up to give back and to be entertained. This meal has nothing but good times attached to it.

¼ cup soy sauce

1 teaspoon lemon juice

⅓ cup Sweet Baby Ray's Barbecue Sauce

1½ to 2 pounds boneless salmon fillets

2 teaspoons sesame seeds

Cracked salt and pepper (optional)

1 Preheat the oven to 375°F. Spray a foil-lined baking pan with a cooking spray, such as PAM.

2 Mix together the soy sauce, lemon juice, and barbecue sauce and rub it on the salmon.

3 Sprinkle sesame seeds all over the salmon.

4 Add cracked salt and pepper, if using.

5 Bake uncovered for 20 minutes.

COCONUT SHRIMP WITH MANGO CHILI SAUCE

4 SERVINGS

One Sunday my sisters and I were all at our parents' house, sitting at the table cackling at various things when I thought, "I wish I would have cooked for them; we should have dinner." We started having a "Sisters Dinner" once a month. Everyone pitches in, I make the entrée, my sister Emma brings the dessert, and my sister Elise brings the wine. The very first dinner I made everything, but they wouldn't allow me to not let them chip in. That's the way we are. We're very close, protective of each other, and we help one another. This dinner is the perfect way to bond and connect with each other, because as we age we get busier, and so we have to be intentional about staying connected. We do that well.

For the dinner, I always pick a "show-off" dish because I want them to feel like they went to a restaurant and coconut shrimp is my top shrimp dish! It's the perfect way to prepare shrimp. Let me explain: The crispy sweet breading with the chili sauce complements the texture and natural seafood taste that comes from shrimp. You can make it as an appetizer or main fling. Plated or on a kabob, however you like it do it!

CONTINUES

Peanut oil or vegetable oil for frying

1 pound raw shrimp, peeled and deveined

Salt and pepper

½ cup flour

2 eggs, beaten

1 cup panko bread crumbs

1 cup shredded coconut, sweetened or unsweetened will be fine

1 Preheat about 2½ inches of frying oil to 365°F, either in a deep fryer or large heavy-bottomed pot, using a candy thermometer to guage the temp.

2 Pat the shrimp dry with paper towels and season with salt and pepper.

3 Set up the dredge bowls as follows: first bowl is for flour, second is for the beaten eggs, and the third one is for the panko and coconut mixed together. Coat the shrimp, a few at a time, first into the flour, then the eggs , then the panko-coconut mixture.

4 Check the oil temperature and fry in batches 1 to 2 minutes per side, if using a pot. The shrimp should be in a single layer, with plenty of room between them. If using a deep fryer, there is no need to turn them, and they will be done in 2 to 3 minutes. Remove to a paper towel–lined plate to drain.

MAMA, I'M ON TV NOW

From culinary to poetry to visual arts to acting, I was knee-deep into generating a buzz connected to my name.

That buzz began to burden me. Everywhere I went, I met people who could use some inspiration one way or another. I wanted to help them, even if I couldn't. Because here's the thing: I internalized all the trouble and anguish I caused my parents. I felt as if I had to pay them back for all the pain, for all the money lost. To do that, I felt I had to inspire anyone who followed me or saw me. The burden became really heavy, and it just got heavier.

And that, my friend, is a recipe for disaster for a person who has self-destructive tendencies.

In 2012, I began to spiral. I also got pregnant with my son, and that pregnancy was a breaking point. During that time anything you could think of happened: breakups, house arrest (yes, while pregnant I was on house arrest for traffic tickets), eviction, ruining professional relationships, and public embarrassment. I wanted to hide, and I did. I got a job at a bank. During my maternity leave I felt as if I were stuck on an island with God. Truth be told, it was the most peaceful time of my life. Even though I was single with a 14-year-old and a newborn, all of us living in a 564-square-foot shotgun house, I felt *rich*. I had a routine, and it consisted of taking care of the kids, cooking, cleaning, and talking to God. Separate from all art forms.

Every morning at 4 AM the baby would awake, and I'd turn on the television in order to not fall back to sleep. For some reason one of my favorite movies, *You've Got Mail,* was on every morning. I loved the simplicity of the masked communication that old-school dial-up service had; it made me want a pen pal. I wanted to feel the excitement when the envelope pops out of the mailbox. An online dating commercial played on that TV station as well, and I decided to create an account. My very first match was this guy named Chris, who I thought I knew from school, and nothing frightened me more at the time than someone who could have been from my past. We exchanged a few emails, and he asked for my number. I declined out of fear and told him that I just wanted to have a pen pal. What happened next? Yes, you thought right: He stopped talking to me.

I went back to my job at the bank. One day I was at work and a coworker was talking about how she met someone from high school online, and I said, "I met a guy I know from school, but he doesn't know that we know each other." Her immediate response was, "Tell him!" Long story short, I finally asked him if he went to Holy Ghost Catholic School, a small school Uptown New Orleans that my cousin Krystal attended. I was always with Krystal when she went to school events so many of the kids knew me at her school, and they liked me more than the kids at my own school. He said, "Who are you?!" I told him that my cousin Krystal was in his class, and he responded, "YOU'RE THAT GIRL! HER OLDER COUSIN!!!" Well, ladies, guys, y'all, guess what? He remembered who I was because we'd danced together at a dance in maybe the fifth grade, and it was a big deal because he was a nerd who got to dance with one of the cute older cousins of one of the coolest girls at his school.

Why did I dance with him when I danced with no one else? Because I admired his courage to approach me. After that, we corresponded nonstop. I gave him my number without him asking this time. He called immediately. After talking for a bit, I told him that I had to drive to a place I didn't know to perform poetry and to give a small talk. I was a bit nervous because I didn't know the area, and he mentioned he knew the area and offered to bring me. So I accepted. The day comes, I get on stage, and perform. He told me how well I did, and people from the audience kept interrupting him to talk to me. He did something that no one had ever done for me, he told me: "No, no go ahead, do what you've gotta do, I'll be right here." No attitude, no bruised ego, just acceptance.

Welp, after that it was fast-tracked. We only had two or three solo dates for a while because everything we did was centered on the kids. We both focused all of our energy on making sure the children were comfortable with all the newness of the relationship. Everyone hit it off well; even our parents and families were happy we found each other. He proposed by three months, and we were married by six months. A shift happened two days before the wedding, because that's when I got fired from the bank. Don't be sad. I was a horrible teller. The management spent a good amount of time fixing my mistakes and technical errors, so I was astonished that I lasted as long as I did. I went home to my soon-to-be husband and told him the news, and I sat with the wind knocked out of me emotionally and mentioned I'd quickly find another job after the honeymoon.

Chris asked about the credit hours I had left in school, and I told him I didn't know. He responded by saying, "You don't just want to find another job." I knew I could get a scholarship for the arts program from Dillard University, because I'd done plays for them, but I had so many more years with culinary so I went with that. After one semester of crying every day on the ride home because I felt that I would be stuck in the kitchen and still had a craving to entertain, I went to the bursar's office to see about classes. The girl at the front desk looked at the computer confused, so confused that I got scared and asked, "What's wrong?!" She said, "We need to go to the dean's office." The dean is now looking puzzled, and she finally broke the silence and said, "Toya, you don't have any classes left to take, you're actually supposed to graduate with this semester's class. I don't know how we missed this!" I leapt so high my glasses flew off and broke. Looking back it was symbolism. My vision for myself and my intellectual worth would never be the same.

Graduation happened and I decided, "Okay, Toya, no more hiding now. It's time to step back out into the public eye." I tried out for the TV show *Hell's Kitchen*. And it seemed as if I was going to get picked; I got pretty far in the process. They even got photos of my ID and all that jazz. I texted the production assistant I was working with, who'd basically told me it was a go, and asked about the next steps. He texted back letting me know that they decided to go in a different direction. I was distraught, and let me tell you on this journey through acting and performing I've seen many casting calls and slammed doors. I once had a casting crew make me audition during their lunch, and they were talking and eating while I was doing a monologue. So, yeah, I'm not that tender. This had to happen though. I came out of the sadness and told Chris, "I'm tired of waiting for someone to give me a show. I'm going to make my own." I started my YouTube channel. Chris was

the "camera crew," and we turned our kitchen into a set. I just jumped in, and I knew I'd get better over time but I had to do it myself.

Everyone knew me as an artist only. I was in culinary school for 14 years, off and on, without anyone knowing. The merge was well received and grew over time. That YouTube channel is how I started to gain attention from producers from Food Network. I didn't have many followers, and every big show I was on was with me having less than 5,000 followers, no viral videos or anything. I built my presence with my character and success rate from the viewers. Now, all the paths merged: performance, public speaking, and culinary to become a storm that took over 14 years to brew. It's showtime, baby!

CLASSIC STEAK & LOBSTER

4 TO 6 SERVINGS

A recipe for classic steak and lobster was my very first YouTube video. That YouTube channel grew Chris and I up quickly as professionals and as a couple. Making the videos was centered on teamwork and finding a harmony. We'd turn the kitchen into a set, and we'd film for hours trying to get everything right. I was aiming to center my channel on teaching people how to make restaurant classics at home if going out was too expensive for them. Whichever dish Chris raved about eating, I'd learn how to cook it so he could have it anytime he wanted. I'd stare at it until I could see it happening in my mind, and then I'd create it. I owe a lot to this particular meal. It was the beginning of me ironing out my kinks in my on-camera presence. I'm forever grateful.

FOR THE LOBSTER

6 (3-ounce) raw lobster tails,
    defrosted if frozen1 cup
    (2 sticks)
½ cup (1 stick) cold salted
    butter, cut into 1-tablespoon
    pieces
3 garlic cloves, minced
½ teaspoon Cajun seasoning,
    more if needed
¼ cup panko bread crumbs
1 teaspoon chopped parsley

FOR THE STEAK

2 teaspoons coarse salt
Cracked black pepper
2 pounds New York strip steaks
3 garlic cloves, bruised
2 tablespoons butter
1 tablespoon chopped parsley

TO MAKE THE LOBSTER

1   Preheat the oven to 350°F and rinse off the lobster tails. Place them
    on a plate or tray that you can use to prep the tails.

2   With a butter knife, starting at the top, separate the meat from the
    shell, leaving a piece of the tail connected (see photograph). To do
    this, gently slide the knife between the meat and the shell. Then,
    while holding the tail firmly with one hand, repeat the motion all
    around the shell until it's completed, still leaving the tip of the tail
    connected to the shell.

3   Next we're going to prepare the lobster tail meat to sit on top of
    the shell. With kitchen shears, cut the top of the shell down the
    center, stopping at the tail fan. Gently spread the shell open with
    one hand and with the other gently wiggle the meat through the
    opening of the shell. At this point allow the shell to close and lay
    the tail meat on top of the shell.

4   Melt the butter. Mix in the garlic and Cajun seasoning.

5   Brush the lobster tails with the butter-garlic mixture. Top with
    the panko and parsley and bake for 15 minutes. Once they're done,
    you can add extra butter and a little extra seasoning, if you like.

TO MAKE THE STEAK

1   Salt and pepper the steaks on both sides and allow them to come to
    an even temperature by sitting them on a plate on the countertop
    for 25 minutes.

2   Heat a large cast-iron skillet until it's very hot and almost smoking.
    Place the steaks in the really hot cast-iron skillet. Sear the first side
    of the steak for 2 minutes. Once you do the initial sear on one side,
    bring the temp to medium.

3   Flip the steaks, add the garlic, butter, and parsley. Spoon the butter
    over the meat and cook until it reaches your desired done point.
    (Use a meat thermometer to measure: for medium-rare, a ther-
    mometer should read 135°F; medium, 140°F; medium-well, 145°F.)
    Let the steak rest for 5 mintues.

FRIED RAVIOLI WITH TASSO CREAM

4 TO 6 SERVINGS

There's a couple different versions of this recipe going around the city, but this one is a favorite of mine. This dish has been a part of many of my celebrations or special moments. My very first television appearance on a major network was snagged by this recipe. Yep, deep-fried ravioli was one of the few recipes I submitted to the culinary producers for the Food Network show Guy's Grocery Games. *I felt it was the perfect recipe to help me get picked, and it did! Guy Fieri's set wowed me. The culture on the set was warm, and no one treated us as if we were insignificant. I knew that it would be a quality I'd store in my mind to have on my own set one day. He was the perfect first culinary celebrity to meet. Just another good omen to confirm I was on the right path.*

2 cups flour

1 tablespoon salt

¼ cup milk

2 eggs

2 cups Italian bread crumbs

4 cups grapeseed oil

1 (16-ounce) package fresh
     ravioli

1 tablespoon butter

2 cups chopped smoked tasso

1 bundle of green onions,
     chopped

1 sweet onion, diced

2 tablespoons minced garlic

4 cups heavy cream

3 tablespoons cornstarch

1 tablespoon smoked paprika

Salt and cracked pepper

Chopped parsley for garnish

1   Set up your dredging station as follows: bowl one is for the flour and salt; bowl two is for the milk and eggs, whisked together; bowl three is for the bread crumbs.

2   Add all of the grapeseed oil to a large pan deep enough to fry ravioli, bring to a medium-high heat.

3   Once the oil is hot enough to fry, begin prepping your ravioli, coating it in the flour first, egg mixture second, and bread crumbs last, then fry. The ravioli is precooked, so you're frying them enough to get golden. It will only take maybe 2 minutes per batch. Repeat the steps until they're all fried.

4   In a large skillet over medium-high heat, add the butter and begin to sauté the tasso, both onions, and garlic for 5 to 7 minutes, until fragrant and caramelized.

5   Add the heavy cream and immediately whisk in the cornstarch at a medium temperature. You will notice that it's thickening.

6   Add the paprika and salt and pepper to taste. Remove from heat and begin to plate the meal, garnishing with parsley. Enjoy!

PANCETTA PANCAKES

4 SERVINGS

For my second challenge on the Food Network show Guy's Grocery Games, I had to do everything with the letter P for my meal. Running around the store I found pancetta, and I immediately thought of pancakes with pancetta drippings and bits in the center, and I said, "Boom, pancetta pancakes!" It was perfectly salty-and-sweet delicious. I was so nervous about hitting the mark, but I did. I realized that my professor and mentor from college Chef Ruth Varisco was right: I was made for all of this.

1½ cups all-purpose flour

2 tablespoons sugar

2 teaspoons baking powder

½ teaspoon baking soda

½ teaspoon salt

1¼ cups milk

2 eggs

2 tablespoons vegetable oil

1 teaspoon vanilla

3 ounces pancetta, diced or
   thinly sliced

1 In a bowl, mix together all the dry ingredients except the pancetta.

2 Pour in each of the wet ingredients while stirring and mix well.

3 Use a small ladle or a ¼ or ½ measuring cup, depending on the size that you prefer, and ladle the pancake batter for each pancake.

4 Before flipping, sprinkle a teaspoon of pancetta all over the pancake. Or if the pancetta is thin-cut sliced, add one slice pancetta in the center of the pancake.

5 Once it's time to flip, the pancetta will begin to release its fat while it's cooking on the other side. You'll know it's time to flip the pancake when you begin to see little bubbles popping all over the pancake. That means the other side is golden.

BLOODY MARY SHRIMP & GRITS

4 SERVINGS

Honey, I have an interesting relationship with shrimp and grits. It was the meal that got me eliminated from the show Food Network Star *and the same meal that got me advanced to the finals on the* Home & Family *show on Hallmark Channel. It wasn't intentional either; it just panned out like that. I believe it was a touch of destiny, like a rainbow after a heavy storm. This is a different recipe than the usual one, and it's more of an ode to the city that makes something normal extravagant. We are known for how crazy our Bloody Marys can get, and I decided to combine that with the shrimp and grits. It is amazing!*

1 cup stone-ground grits (if it's an appetizer or 2 cups grits if it's an entrée)
Water (see step 1)
Milk (see step 1)
1 tablespoon salt, more for seasoning the shrimp
1 pound jumbo shrimp, peeled and deveined
Pepper
2 tablespoons butter
½ cup chopped onions
¼ cup chopped celery
¼ cup chopped bell pepper, more for serving
1 teaspoon chopped garlic
1 tablespoon tomato paste
1 cup tomato juice
1 shot of vodka, or add 1 tablespoon at a time until you have the desired taste
2 cups chopped cherry tomatoes for topping
Cajun seasoning
Olives or other toppings (optional)

1 Cook the grits as the package instructs except replace half of the water with milk. For example: if the instructions say to add 4 cups water, you'll add 2 cups water and 2 cups milk.

2 Because dairy swells when brought to a high temp, as soon as the liquid starts to smoke (just before boiling), whisk in the grits with 1 tablespoon salt and cook as directed.

3 For the sauce: Sauté the shrimp, seasoned with salt and pepper, in a large skillet greased with olive oil spray for 4 to 6 minutes. Remove the shrimp from the pan and set aside. In the same skillet, add the butter, veggies, and garlic and sauté until tender, about 5 minutes.

4 Add the tomato paste and juice and return the shrimp to the pan. Add the vodka a little at a time to gauge the taste and Cajun seasoning to taste.

5 Spoon the sauce over the grits for each serving. Top with extra peppers, chopped tomatoes, olives, or anything you want to add to jazz up your dish.

"You've got to decide if you're going to be a sizzle in the pan or a slow cook." —CHEF KEVIN BELTON

The entertainment world was a true culture shock. It caused me to travel and encounter other culinarians who lived completely different lives. Some of the chefs I met were Le Cordon Bleu trained, studied in Italy, lived in Paris, worked at five-star restaurants, basically doing all the things that I was not familiar with. In between filming on the shows, talking to the chefs was a little tough. I know, one could say, "Toya, these shows were competitions; they don't want to be friends." But that wasn't the issue. If I couldn't contribute to the conversation about a visit to Napa or talk about the places I've been, then I was immediately overlooked. When I first started out on the cooking shows, I had never been to a white tablecloth restaurant. As a kid, we cooked at home. As a grown woman, I was a single mother with tight funds, and honestly I never thought of eating out much because it wasn't an option. When I got married, we were a couple with three children with one income on a tight budget. In order to keep up, you better believe that I studied all the culinary shows and watched every interview; I did whatever I could to be prepared for that world. I watched to see how they build stories, how the stress could make the contestants respond and appear to viewers. Quickly I realized it was more about entertainment, and about how to display myself the way I wanted the world to see me. I learned something very valuable from studying celebrity interviews: Everyone in the entertainment business makes a "no-matter-what decision" in some way. For example, my no-matter-what decision was: "No matter what, I want to consistently stay faithful to my character, and be solid and true." This was more important than anything else, because my kids and many other kids would be looking at me or up to me.

I knew that I may not be able out-cook them with ingredients I'd never seen before, but I could focus on my personality. I could be myself unapologetically, inspiring others to be themselves, breaking down fear centered on cooking, and teaching others how to heal. Appearance by appearance, I gained more confidence knowing that one day all of these genuine intentional steps would take me far. I finally shook off my "new kid on the block" jitters.

BEIGNETS WITH RASPBERRY COULIS

4 TO 6 SERVINGS

I was in a competition on the Hallmark Channel's Home & Family *show in 2017. I went on this show shortly after I got eliminated from* The Next Food Network Star. *After I got eliminated, I didn't want to see a TV set until the reunion show, but I changed my mind, because I had a sneaking suspicion that I was pregnant again. So I agreed to do the Hallmark show, and I found out the night before I went to California for the competition that I was right: Chris and I were about to have a new baby! So that meant us having a new set of needs, and the money I could earn from the competition would make it all easier to handle. One of the days after the filming was over, one of the competitors, Kelley Wolf, walked right up to me and said that she just knew I was going to win. Kelley had no clue about the uncomfortable encounters I had with contestants on other shows; she was just that raw, honest, and genuine. She didn't know all the newness that was happening in my life, and how any new path could make me feel insecure. I was so insecure after my last experience that Kelley's words stuck with me and kept me pushing. (Kelley and I are still rocking till this day.) The very next day I won $25,000 with this dish. That was the beginning of a relationship with the cast and crew that still pumps warm blood today. The* Home & Family *show cast was the most loving cast. For five years I had the privilege of cooking alongside some of the sweetest spirits, Debbie Matenopoulos and Cameron Mathison. We'd be in the kitchen trading stories and creating good memories. Even though the show came to an end, we still keep in touch. Agreeing to go on this show was one of the best choices I've made concerning my career, and they'll always have a place in my heart.*

FOR THE BEIGNETS

3 cups flour
½ teaspoon nutmeg
½ teaspoon cinnamon
1 teaspoon salt
1 cup milk

2 tablespoons butter
1 tablespoon brown sugar
1 tablespoon granulated sugar
1 (0.75-ounce) package yeast
1 egg
Powdered sugar
grapeseed oil for frying

FOR THE RASPBERRY COULIS

1 pint raspberries
4 teaspoons sugar

CONTINUES

TO MAKE THE BEIGNETS

1. In a small bowl, mix together the flour, nutmeg, cinnamon, and salt.

2. Heat the milk (steaming but not boiling).

3. Place the butter and sugars in a large mixing bowl. Pour the scalding milk over the top of them.

4. Stir the milk so that the butter melts and the sugar dissolves.

5. Add the yeast and stir it in.

6. Add the egg and half of the dry ingredients to the large bowl and beat well.

7. Add the rest of the dry ingredients and mix well.

8. Place the dough on a floured counter and knead 2 to 3 minutes, until it is soft and pliable.

9. Place your kneaded dough into a large greased bowl. Cover and let rise for about 1 hour, or until doubled in size.

10. Place the dough onto a floured counter and flour a rolling pin. Roll the dough out to about ¼ inch thick.

11. Cut the dough into 3-inch squares. It should be a dozen squares or a few extra.

12. Place the dough pieces on a greased cookie sheet and cover with greased (I use PAM cooking spray) plastic wrap. Allow them to rise for 30 minutes to 1 hour, until they have almost doubled in size.

13. In a large skillet with 3½ inches of oil, fry the dough 1 to 2 minutes each side over medium-high heat. Sprinkle generously with powdered sugar.

TO MAKE THE RASPBERRY COULIS

1. Place the berries and sugar in the blender and blend until it's completely smooth.

2. Spoon the sauce onto the bottom of the plate before adding the beignets.

BROWNED BUTTER SCALLOPS

2 SERVINGS

I was deep into the interview process for one of the shows I went on, and the producer called me and said, "Hey, we need more photos of different types of meals." I didn't have many they could use, because the food photos I had were of the stuff I'd cooked for my family. I asked him what they wanted to see, and he responded, "Maybe something upscale, like scallops." I thought, "What?" I'd never even had scallops before! I went to the store, and because it was my first time buying them, the price caught me off guard. I gave myself one shot, because for damn sure I wasn't going to blow my grocery budget trying to impress the producers. I kept it as simple as I could, because I knew that there's nothing that butter, garlic, salt, and pepper can't fix! And it came out perfect!

1 pound scallops
Kosher salt and freshly ground
   black pepper
6 tablespoons salted butter
1 tablespoon olive oil
1 garlic clove, minced

1 Remove the small side muscle (the tough little connector piece) from the scallops, rinse with cold water, and thoroughly pat dry. Sprinkle with salt and pepper to taste. Set aside.

2 Make the browned butter: Melt the butter in a small saucepan over medium heat and cook for about 4 minutes until it begins to brown. Set aside.

3 Heat the olive oil in a large skillet over medium-high heat. Working in batches, add the scallops to the skillet in a single layer and cook, flipping once, until golden brown and translucent in the center, 1 to 2 minutes per side. Place the scallops on a plate, set aside, and keep warm.

4 Reduce the heat for the large skillet to medium-low. Add the browned butter, garlic, and sauté until fragrant, about 3 minutes. Add the scallops back to the skillet; spoon the butter over them quickly, so the scallops don't overcook, for about a minute.

5 Serve immediately over a salad or keep it simple and make it an appetizer.

BUTTERMILK-ROASTED CHICKEN WITH BLACK TRUFFLE POTATOES

4 SERVINGS

When I was on the show **The Next Food Network Star,** *I was eliminated during the second round. After you're eliminated, your time on the show isn't over: You're required to come back for the reunion and finale of the show. The winner was announced and the filming wrapped. That chapter was closed officially. All of us (including the other contestants) were drained and ready to unwind. We were all in the van being transported to a restaurant, because everyone wanted to go out to eat. I cringed because at this point I was a little past eight weeks pregnant, and only a few things didn't make me nauseous. At that time I pretty much could have eaten French toast and hash browns three times a day thanks to my pregnancy cravings. They settled on a spot. I hadn't given much input because my budget for eating was razor thin; as long as they were staying away from fine dining I would be okay. I had just won some money from my appearance on Hallmark Channel, but we were in the process of selling our house so that we could get a house with an extra room and space, plus get a new car to fit everyone. All of this was happening within a matter of a few months because we wanted to be settled before the baby arrived.*

We walked into the restaurant, got seated, and the first thing I focused my eyes on was the prices. We were in Brooklyn, New York, so I knew the prices would be a little higher than usual. Typically when I travel I get takeout from a fast food spot or I get something that keeps the costs down, but I'd just spent the entire day with these people during filming, and this dinner was probably the last night I'd see them. So I combed the menu to find out what I was going to blow a part of my food budget on, and I ordered a chicken and truffle potato dish. It was textbook perfect, from the juices of the tender chicken to the smooth velvety feel of the roasted potatoes. Needless to say I loved it so much that I re-created it!

The night went a lot better than I imagined. I'm sure it was because the competitive edge was off, and we were all over it as well. There was no drama from reliving our conflicts. No one talked about being eliminated. We just ate and laughed. We went to a bar down the street after and that's when I dropped the pregnancy bomb, because of course I'm in the bar ordering a Cherry Coke—an odd choice given the circumstances. The few I told were very excited. It was a really good moment. It felt genuine, and out of all the things that I experienced with them, that's what I held on to the most.

FOR THE CHICKEN

1 whole chicken, rinsed inside
     and out
7 cups buttermilk
10 to 15 garlic cloves, bruised
½ cup salt
¼ cup black pepper
2 teaspoons poultry seasoning
2 cups water
1 onion, chopped
1 bell pepper, chopped
Cajun seasoning
1 lemon wedge
½ cup (1 stick) butter

FOR THE BLACK TRUFFLE POTATOES

4 pounds small to medium
     Yukon Gold potatoes, peeled
3 tablespoons butter
⅛ teaspoon black truffle oil
Truffle salt

TO MAKE THE CHICKEN

1 In a large 2-gallon ziplock bag or a very large bowl, add the rinsed chicken, buttermilk, garlic, salt, pepper, and poultry seasoning.

2 Close it and gently shake it slightly, mixing it all around. Marinade it for 1 to 2 days in the fridge. When it's time to bake, remove the chicken from the fridge and sit it on the countertop (still in the marinade) to bring it to room temp so it will cook evenly.

3 Preheat the oven to 375°F. Line a roasting pan with foil, add the water, onion, and bell pepper, and then add the rack to the pan.

4 Rinse off the chicken because the milk will cause the chicken to turn dark quickly while baking. Discard the marinade.

5 Place the whole chicken on the rack. With kitchen twine, tie both drumsticks together with a tight knot. This will help the breasts cook evenly. Sprinkle with Cajun seasoning before baking.

6 Add the lemon wedge to a bowl with the butter. Melt the butter in the microwave with the lemon wedge and set aside. We will baste the chicken with this.

7 Bake the chicken for 50 minutes, basting it with the lemon butter halfway through.

8 The chicken will be done at 165°F if you're using a thermometer.

9 Let it rest for 20 minutes before cutting.

TO MAKE THE BLACK TRUFFLE POTATOES

1 Bring a large pot of water to boil over high heat. Add the whole potatoes and cook for 20 minutes. Remove and drain.

2 Chop the potatoes into chunks and place in a ricer or food mill and puree.

3 Gently stir in the melted butter and drizzle the black truffle oil on top. Add the truffle salt to taste and gently stir again to blend well. Serve and enjoy!

EXPENSIVE ASS SALAD

4 SERVINGS

I've run across a lot of expensive stuff that was "okay," but this damn salad is so good, I never really want a salad any other way! Let's not forget the name of the salad though: it lives up to it. It's the "Mama, I made it!" of the salad world. It's filling, the flavors are delicate and well balanced, and honey, the cash money feel of the champagne caviar vinaigrette is priceless in flavor. It's definitely a celebratory meal indeed.

2 raw lobster tails removed
    from the shell
1 cup (2 sticks) plus 2
    tablespoons butter
2 tablespoons plus ½ teaspoon
    lemon juice
½ teaspoon coarse salt, more
    for seasoning
½ teaspoon black pepper, more
    for seasoning
8 ounces lump crabmeat
Cajun seasoning
½ pound large scallops
2 tablespoons avocado oil
½ cup olive oil
¼ cup white balsamic vinegar
½ cup canola oil
1 ounce caviar of your choice,
    more if desired
½ cup champagne of your
    choice
Spring mix salad greens
Edible gold foil

TO MAKE THE LOBSTER

1 In a small pot over medium heat, add the 1 cup butter, 2 tablespoons lemon juice, ¼ teaspoon of the salt, and black pepper. Once the butter is melted, place the lobster tails in the butter to cook for 2 to 3 minutes, until the meat is no longer translucent.

2 Take the lobster tails, chop them into chunks, add a couple of spoons of butter, place them on a piece of foil, and pull up all the sides to make a pocket to hold in the heat while you get everything ready. Set aside.

TO MAKE THE CRABMEAT

Sprinkle ½ teaspoon lemon juice and the Cajun seasoning to taste to season the crabmeat. Divide into two portions and set aside.

TO MAKE THE SCALLOPS

Remove the small side muscle (the tough little connector piece) from the scallops, rinse with cold water, and thoroughly pat dry. Lightly salt and pepper the scallops. In a medium pan, sear the first side for 2 minutes with avocado oil over medium heat, flip them, and then add 2 tablespoons butter and cook for an additional minute or so while basting with butter. Create another foil pocket for the scallops. Set aside.

CONTINUES

TO MAKE THE DRESSING

Add the olive oil, vinegar, canola, and ¼ teaspoon of the salt and whisk until a little frothy. Fold in the caviar and champagne. Pour into whatever jar or glass you're using for the dressing.

TO ASSEMBLE THE SALAD

1 Add the greens to the bowls, evenly distribute the seafood, add extra caviar, or don't, it's all up to you. Every time I pour the dressing I give it a little shake.

2 Easily apply the edible gold to the scallops and lobster as the package directs you. Serve and enjoy!

CRAB CAKES WITH
LEMON CAPER CREAM

4 SERVINGS

I was well prepared for being sequestered, without TV or cell phone access, for a month or so during the filming of The Next Food Network Star. But eating the same thing every night through room service was a different ball game. And since everyone was making room service orders at the same time, and because we were all on the same floor for the most part, by the time the food got to me it was lukewarm. And if they forgot the salt and pepper I ordered, I was in trouble. Just picture this: I'm from a city where food can calm a storm, and after a hard day I could go anywhere to get a piping hot, good, well-seasoned meal. So a lukewarm, lightly seasoned meal on a tray wasn't cutting it. Ya girl was struggling. Luckily, I stumbled on a gem on the menu: crab cakes! So I ate the same thing for dinner every night, but I'll say this: It was so good that after a long day I looked forward to this meal. You'd think because of that experience I wouldn't ever want to see a crab cake again, but it's the direct opposite. I actually love them a little more because it was something I took solace in. It also helped that they were the good kind of crab cakes, with flaky lumps of crabmeat and the least amount of breading so that the quality of the crab could shine and the flavor could punch! You can find good crab cakes all around New Orleans because you can count on New Orleanians to have any seafood dish down to a science.

FOR THE CRAB CAKES

1 pound lump crabmeat
½ cup panko bread crumbs
1 egg
3 tablespoons mayonnaise
Juice of 1 small lemon
1 tablespoon fresh minced
    parsley
2 teaspoons Worcestershire
    sauce
1 teaspoon Dijon mustard
Zest of ½ lemon
1 teaspoon salt
½ teaspoon black pepper
¼ teaspoon cayenne pepper
2 to 3 tablespoons canola oil for
    cooking

FOR THE LEMON CAPER CREAM

1 tablespoon butter
1 tablespoon olive oil
4 garlic cloves, minced
⅔ cup heavy cream
2 tablespoons capers, drained
1 teaspoon freshly squeezed
    lemon juice, more if desired
Salt

TO MAKE THE CRAB CAKES

1 Check every lump of meat, carefully feeling around for any left-over shell fragments. You don't need to break it apart, just check around the lumps.

2 Mix all the ingredients for the crab cakes except for the crabmeat and oil in a bowl and whisk well.

3 Add the crabmeat and mix it well. Break up some of the lumps and leave others in chunks.

4 Use an ice cream scoop to spoon out equal amounts of crab mixture. Shape the patties but don't press them tight, just enough to form the shape of a patty.

5 Preheat a medium nonstick skillet over medium to medium-high heat and add the oil.

6 Let the oil heat up until hot and add the crab cakes. Do not move them after you place them in the pan until ready to flip. Cook the crab cakes for 4 to 5 minutes per side.

TO MAKE THE LEMON CAPER CREAM

1 In a medium skillet, heat the butter, olive oil, and garlic on medium heat.

2 Cook for about a minute, until the garlic softens. Add the heavy cream, bring to a boil, and cook for a couple of minutes, or until the sauce thickens a bit.

3 Remove from heat. Stir in the capers and lemon juice. Taste and add more lemon juice, if needed, and salt to taste. Keep covered until serving.

SIMPLE TUNA TARTARE

BEET TARTARE

SALMON TARTARE

BEEF TARTARE

TARTARE 4 WAYS

4 SERVINGS

Mama would always say that I was a "Mikey," like my father. For those of you who've never heard of that term, it comes from an old Life cereal commercial, and the saying was, "Give it to Mikey, he'll eat anything." The commercial actually said, "Give it to Mikey. He won't eat it, he hates everything." But over time people turned it around to where he liked everything. My first time eating tartare, this statement popped in my mind. I was in LA at a hotel restaurant, and I let the bartender pick my meal. When it came out I thought, "Okay, I'm gonna see this through." I laughed on the inside, tried it, and without hesitation I loved it. I loved how light I felt after, fulfilled but not full. The experience was narrated by the quality of the ingredients. That's what made it memorable. I remember thinking that the tartare was so simple and fresh, that making it at home for a gathering would be a breeze, and that it would definitely elevate the menu. If you're going to jump out the gate slinging tartare on the table, you'd better come out swinging. Give it to them four ways.

SIMPLE TUNA TARTARE

2 tablespoons low-sodium soy sauce

1 tablespoon sesame oil

2 teaspoons fresh lime juice

1 teaspoon ginger paste or 1 teaspoon grated fresh ginger

1 pound fresh ahi tuna, sushi-grade

½ medium avocado, diced

3 tablespoons white onion, very thinly sliced

½ to 1 jalapeño, deseeded and minced

¼ cup finely chopped cilantro

1 teaspoon toasted sesame seeds, more for serving

Lime wedges for serving

1 Combine the soy sauce, sesame oil, lime juice, and ginger paste in a small bowl, then whisk well. Set aside.

2 Using a very sharp knife, cut the tuna into ⅛-inch dice, trimming away any sinew or skin. Place the tuna in a large mixing bowl.

3 Add the avocado, onion, jalapeño (half if you like it mild or the full pepper for a bit more heat), cilantro, and sesame seeds. Pour the marinade on top, then toss to thoroughly coat.

4 Stir the tartare. Serve with an extra sprinkle of sesame seeds and lime wedges.

BEET TARTARE

2 pounds beets, precooked
1 jalapeño pepper, seeded and
    minced
3 tablespoons thinly sliced
    green onions
1 tablespoon rice wine vinegar
2 teaspoons soy sauce
2 teaspoons grated fresh ginger
1 teaspoon sesame oil
4 avocados, diced
¼ cup chopped fresh cilantro
2 tablespoons lime juice
1 teaspoon kosher salt
2 teaspoons black sesame seeds,
    or to taste
Circular or square mold

1   Cut the beets into small dice. Mix the diced beets with the jalapeño pepper, green onions, vinegar, soy sauce, ginger, and sesame oil together in a bowl; cover with plastic wrap and marinate the beets for 20 to 30 minutes.

2   Gently stir the avocado, cilantro, lime juice, and kosher salt together in a separate bowl, being careful not to mash the avocado.

3   Using a circular or square mold, scoop a ¼ cup beet tartare into the mold, then add ¼ cup avocado mixture. Gently remove from the mold onto the plate. Keep repeating the process until all the tartare is used. Sprinkle black sesame seeds on top and serve.

SALMON TARTARE

1½ pounds salmon fillet
2 ripe avocados
4 chive sprigs
1 teaspoon lemon juice
½ teaspoon lime juice
1 tablespoon olive oil
⅛ teaspoon sea salt
¼ teaspoon crushed pepper
1 tablespoon toasted sesame
    seeds
Pastry ring mold

1   Slice the salmon into small, bite-sized cubes. Chop the avocado into thin slices.

2   Chop the chives and mix them with the chopped salmon and avocado.

3   Sprinkle with the lemon juice, lime juice, and olive oil. Add the salt and pepper. Then keep it cool for 3 hours.

4   Garnish the tartare with toasted sesame seeds. Mold the salmon into a pastry ring and place on a plate. Carefully remove the mold and serve immediately.

BEEF TARTARE

3 medium oil-packed anchovy
   fillets (optional, adjust salt if
   added), rinsed and minced
2 teaspoons brined capers,
   drained and rinsed
3 teaspoons Dijon mustard
2 large egg yolks
10 ounces USDA prime
   beef tenderloin, cut into
   small dice, covered, and
   refrigerated
2 tablespoons finely chopped
   red onion
2 tablespoons finely chopped
   Italian parsley leaves
4 teaspoons olive oil
3 dashes hot sauce (such as
   Tabasco)
4 dashes Worcestershire sauce
¾ teaspoon crushed chile
   flakes (optional)
Salt
Freshly ground pepper
Toast points or french fries for
   serving

1 Combine the anchovies (if using), capers, and mustard in a non-
reactive bowl. Using a fork or the back of a spoon, mash the ingredients until evenly combined. Mix in the egg yolks.

2 Use a rubber spatula to fold the remaining ingredients, except the
toast or fries, into the mustard mixture until thoroughly combined.
Season well with salt and black pepper. Serve immediately with
toast points or french fries.

EXPENSIVE ASS DEVILED EGGS

4 SERVINGS

I think if "Can I talk my shit again?" was an egg, it would be these expensive ass deviled eggs. I have so much fun making these eggs! I designed these eggs with my artwork in mind. Shapes and textures, lines and dots, all of it was edible art. The day the photos of the eggs were taken was the last day of shooting, and Sam (our photographer) and I stared at the plate and admired each component and placement. I could have those shots framed. They represent this next place I'm going to creatively. Fearless and fly. The flavor is through the roof, and you guessed it, you can pair this with the Expensive Ass Salad (page 131) and make it an expensive ass night!

8 hard-boiled eggs
¼ cup black truffle mayo
1 teaspoon lemon juice
1 tablespoon finely chopped
  chives, more for garnish
4 ounces lump crabmeat
¼ teaspoon smoked paprika
1 teaspoon Dijon mustard
  (I used Grey Poupon)
⅛ teaspoon salt, more for
  seasoning
⅛ teaspoon cayenne pepper
¼ pound baby scallops
Pepper
1 tablespoon avocado oil
2 teaspoons caviar of your
  choice
4 strips cooked applewood
  bacon, chopped
Edible gold for garnish

1   Slice the eggs in half lengthwise. Remove the yolks neatly, placing the empty whites on a serving platter and the yolks in a bowl for mixing.

2   Add the mayo, lemon juice, chives, crab, paprika, mustard, salt, and cayenne pepper. Mix until well blended; add more salt if needed.

3   Take the filling and stuff it into a piping bag with a large tip, or you can leave it in a bowl and spoon it in; it really depends on the look you want. Set the bag and filling to the side.

4   Lightly season the scallops with salt and pepper. Add the avocado oil to a small skillet over medium heat and get it hot. Sear the scallops; they take maybe 2 minutes total to cook. Set them aside.

5   Stuff the egg yolks, then arrange edible décor (as shown in the photo). Top the eggs with the bacon, scallops, and chives. The bacon and scallops are the best places to apply the gold. Add caviar to each egg and you're set!

CHAPTER FOUR

SIDES AND SOUP

**Red beans and fried chicken
are my favorite meal**

In New Orleans, we eat red beans, white beans, navy beans, and butter beans always with fried or baked chicken or fried fish.

Beans and rice were brought to the city in the late 1700s by French-speaking Haitians fleeing the revolution in Saint-Domingue (modern-day Haiti). They were one of the first groups to rise up against slavery. Trying to find safety they came here. They brought along all of their rich flavors, including Caribbean dishes with beans and rice. Beans are cheap and they stretch, so it took no time for them to become popular. It became a Monday tradition to eat red beans and rice, because Monday was the day women did chores and washed clothes. Washing clothes was a daunting task that took a great deal of the day in the 19th century. In order to carry on with chores and feed the family you needed to cook something that wouldn't need much babysitting. You can imagine what it was like for them.

Today, it takes 3 hours on our fancy stoves to cook red beans until they're buttery smooth, so I'm sure that paints a clear picture of how much time they had to do laundry while the beans cooked. Beans are fairly easy to cook because the technique is simple. But it's a lot like the roux: If you burn them, you have to throw the whole pot away! There's something about beans and the broth that if a bit of it gets burned a scorched taste runs through the entire pot faster than you can say, "I'm sorry."

That tradition of red beans and rice still flows through the streets of New Orleans. Damn near every restaurant will have red beans and rice on the menu. Even if they only have it as a side, you can bet it'll be there.

RED BEANS

6 TO 8 SERVINGS

As a kid if I saw the ingredients for beans out the night before, I got excited because I knew for two or three days I'd have one of my favorite meals for dinner. Now, at almost 40 years old, my mama will text me to tell me, "I made beans, I fixed a container for you." I will pass by a corner store and pick up a few pieces of chicken, swing by my mama's to get the beans, and find a place in the house to hide and eat, just so I won't have to share. I'm sure a lot of people can relate to that feeling of knowing everyone in your house ate, and ate well . . . but if they see you excited about a meal, all of a sudden they want a "taste," which ends with you sharing your glorious solo meal. I don't blame them, I get it. There's just something about that well-seasoned, slightly smoky taste from the beans and the sausage. It's one of the foodways to my heart.

1 pound dried red beans
1 cup chopped onion
½ cup chopped green onion
½ cup chopped celery
½ cup chopped bell pepper
2 pounds andouille sausage
½ pound applewood bacon
1 smoked turkey neck
3 tablespoons chopped garlic
3 quarts stock (veggie, chicken, or pork)
Cajun seasoning
Cooked rice for serving (make whichever rice you like as the package directs)

1   Prep the beans by soaking them in water overnight.

2   In a large pan over medium heat, sauté the onions, celery, and peppers for 8 minutes until caramelized and set aside.

3   Sauté the sausage and bacon at the same time on medium heat in the pot you will be cooking the beans in. Keep them moving by stirring them. (The objective is to get the fat from both in the pot early to influence the flavor and to get the sausage all nice and caramelized.) After 7 minutes, once both are sticky but not overcooked, remove the sausage and bacon and set aside.

4   Add the beans to the pot along with the veggies, 2 quarts (8 cups) of the stock, smoked turkey neck, and garlic. You can add the bacon back in also, but that is optional.

5   Let everything cook down for about an hour and a half uncovered over medium heat. The liquid will decrease. Stir sporadically. Add 2 cups more of the stock at this point, then the sausage (and bacon, if you have not done so already) and allow to cook for another hour. Begin to taste and season with Cajun seasoning to taste. The last 30 minutes is the perfect time to decide what your consistency will be. For thicker red beans, do not add extra liquid. For thinner red beans, add about ½ cup to 1 cup of stock at a time.

CORN BREAD

6 SERVINGS

My father is a whiz with a cast-iron skillet and corn bread. It didn't matter if he was baking it like a cake to be sliced into wedges or squares, or he was making it another way. I'd sometimes see him fry the batter to make small pancakes, and he could make a half dozen or so in minutes to go with white beans or greens. The corn bread we have today is an adaptation of a style made from maize that the Native Americans would grind into a meal and mix with water and salt. As times progressed so did the recipe and ingredients, all of it fluctuating depending on what was available. Slaves relied on the traditional method for making and serving corn bread. It was used as a filler in a way. Traditionally, the corn bread was crumbled up at the bottom of the bowl to sop up the drippings from the collards, for example. It was like the cherry on the top of the meal. It also ended up with the name hoe cakes, which are small, flat corn bread disks fried in a skillet, cooked the same way as a pancake. Corn bread has traveled so far and has changed in so many ways. It's amazing to me how a good bit of our everyday actions and cravings is simply the pulse of history that's still throbbing and evolving.

1 cup all-purpose flour

1 cup yellow cornmeal
(self-rising)

⅔ cup white sugar

1 teaspoon salt

3 ½ teaspoons baking powder
(only if your cornmeal is not
self-rising)

1 egg

1 cup milk

⅓ cup vegetable oil

2 teaspoons butter

2 teaspoons honey

1 Preheat the oven to 400°F.

2 Spray or lightly grease a 9-inch round cake pan or cast-iron skillet. Tip: Lining the pan with foil will help cleanup.

3 In a large bowl, combine the flour, cornmeal, sugar, salt, and baking powder, if needed.

4 Stir in the egg, milk, and vegetable oil until well combined.

5 Pour the batter into the prepared pan.

6 Bake in the preheated oven for 20 to 25 minutes, until a toothpick inserted into the center of the corn bread comes out clean.

7 Butter the top of the corn bread and drizzle a little honey for extra flavor.

CAJUN CORN ON THE COB

6 SERVINGS

My mama always tells a story about how during her pregnancy with me she would buy a bundle of ears of corn, boil them, and eat them all up! There's just something about corn as a side that's comforting. Thanks to this story, I think I know why: In this day and age when everything has been canned and sped up the production ladder, the simplicity of it all is heartwarming and reassuring. Now I bake them in the oven to save time, and there's less cleanup too.

1 cup salted butter, softened, more for serving if desired
1 teaspoon chopped garlic (about 1 clove)
1 tablespoon Cajun seasoning
6 ears corn

1 Preheat the oven to 425°F.

2 Mix the softened butter, garlic, and Cajun seasoning, and set it aside for later. (Congratulations, you've probably just made your first compound butter! I'll explain more later.)

3 Remove the husks and silk of each ear of corn.

4 Place each ear on a separate piece of foil. Before wrapping each ear in the foil, brush the corn with the butter mixture, then seal it and place it on a baking sheet. The sheet of foil wrapped around will aid in the roasting and the speed of cooking.

5 Bake for 25 minutes.

6 Remove and add more butter if desired when serving.

Compound Butters

Compounds can make the world go 'round! In culinary school we made compound butters at the top of the semester. I guess you can say that was sort of a needed ingredient on our class supply list. Lemon butter, garlic, Cajun, cinnamon butter . . . the list can go on. You don't have to be a culinary student to have these on hand to make cooking easier and tastier. Compound butter is amazing with breakfast bagels!

Now, the formula is pretty easy: just 1 cup (2 sticks) of softened butter and the seasoning or flavor of your choice! Sweet or savory. You can make a compound butter and freeze it for up to 3 months! You can find cool molds online too.

GARLIC PARMESAN BUTTER: Mix together 1 cup of room-temperature butter, 6 tablespoons of shredded or grated Parmesan cheese, and 6 garlic cloves, minced.

CINNAMON BUTTER: Mix together 1 cup of room-temperature butter and 1½ teaspoons of cinnamon.

SMOKY FETA CRUMBLE BUTTER: Mix together 1 cup of room-temperature butter, 1½ tablespoons of smoked paprika, and 6 tablespoons of feta crumbles.

LEMON PEPPER BUTTER: Mix together 1 cup of room-temperature butter, 1 teaspoon of lemon zest, 1 tablespoon of lemon juice, and 1 tablespoon of cracked black pepper.

GARLIC
PARMESAN
BUTTER

CINNAMON
BUTTER

SMOKY FETA
CRUMBLE
BUTTER

LEMON PEPPER BUTTER

FRIED OKRA

4 SERVINGS

I love that the fast food chains in New Orleans feature fried okra as an option instead of fries. If you don't like it sautéed or in gumbo, try it fried! With the crisp cornmeal coating and Cajun seasoning, there's nothing slimy here. It's a perfect addition to a fish fry—it's amazing. I like adding fried okra as a topping on my own plate of étouffée! Give it a try!

Vegetable oil for frying
1 pound okra
1½ cups buttermilk
1 egg
2 cups yellow cornmeal
2 cups self-rising flour
2 teaspoons salt
1 teaspoon Cajun seasoning

1 Add the oil to the fryer and preheat the fryer to 375°F, or if using a skillet, heat the oil.

2 Cut the okra either into ½-inch slices or cut them in half lengthwise; set aside. Whisk together the buttermilk and egg in a shallow bowl; set aside. In a separate shallow bowl, combine the cornmeal with the flour, salt, and Cajun seasoning.

3 Once the oil is hot, prepare the okra for frying: Dip the pieces first into the buttermilk, let excess buttermilk drip off, and then dredge in the flour mixture. Fry in batches for 3 or 4 minutes, just until golden brown; don't crowd the skillet. Let drain on paper towels. Serve hot.

SUCCOTASH

6 TO 8 SERVINGS

Growing up, I remember that succotash was just a freestyle mix of veggies and stuff we had in the house. I had no clue of its history and the travels it took to get to my table. From the hands of the Indigenous people this came. Of course the natives here in New Orleans put their own spin on it, but we remember where it came from. Full flavors and good food for the heart and soul.

4 tablespoons butter
1 sweet onion, chopped
2 bell peppers, chopped
½ celery stalk, chopped
1 tablespoon chopped garlic
2 cups cubed ham
1 (14-ounce) can lima beans, drained
2 (14-ounce) cans diced tomatoes
1 bay leaf
2 cups chopped okra
1 pound raw shrimp, peeled and deveined
Cajun seasoning
Cooked rice

1   Melt the butter in a large, deep skillet or Dutch oven over medium-high heat. Add the onions, bell peppers, celery, garlic, and cubed ham and cook, stirring occasionally, about 10 minutes, until caramelized.

2   Add the beans, tomatoes, bay leaf, and okra and simmer on low for 10 minutes.

3   Add the shrimp and allow to cook for 8 to 10 minutes until the shrimp are firm.

4   Season with the Cajun seasoning to taste and serve hot over rice.

RED GRAVY

6 TO 8 SERVINGS

Red gravy is a strong contender in the "make it stretch" competition. Growing up, my mama would make it with sausage or meatballs, and I swear her red gravy was so damn good you'd want to lick the plate. As I got older, I discovered that Italians make red gravy as well. My mama would make a gumbo pot of red gravy and freeze half of it for another time—she was so strategic with her cooking for the week. To me, as a kid, she just seemed like a magician, because she made everything appear so easy. But now, as an adult and a mother, I see that her magic was so much planning and thoughtfulness. Considering her and my father's work schedule, and that they also had to come up with lunch and dinner meals, too, taking something out of the freezer instead of cooking would have been a godsend at the end of a tiring workday. That was our "fast food." This red gravy base can be used with turkey meatballs, sausage, veggies, or plain with any pasta you like.

1 cup vegetable oil

1 cup flour

3 ounces (6 tablespoons) tomato paste

4 cups tomato sauce

6 cups stock (chicken or vegetable), more if needed

2 sweet onions, peeled and chopped

1 bell pepper, chopped

1 celery stalk, chopped

1 bay leaf

1 teaspoon Italian seasoning

3 teaspoons chopped garlic

2 teaspoons sugar

Salt and pepper

1 Let's make a roux. Heat the oil in a large skillet, add the flour, and cook stirring constantly over medium heat until it becomes a peanut butter color, then remove from heat.

2 Add the tomato paste and sauce, mix well, and return to heat.

3 Begin adding the stock: add 3 of the cups and whisk around. We're trying to find the consistency and thickness you'd prefer to have. Some like it thin, some like it thick. If you add all 6 cups and you think you want it thinner, add more stock until you're satisfied. Don't worry about it creating a lot, you can freeze the rest and use it as a base.

4 Add the chopped veggies, bay leaf, Italian seasoning, garlic, and sugar.

5 Begin to salt and pepper to taste. Let it simmer for 20 minutes over medium-low heat so that the flavors can "marry." Taste the gravy. If you can taste the individual flavors of the ingredients, then you need to simmer it more. Taste it every 5 to 7 minutes to see if you need to go longer. It should taste like it's all one unit.

6 When the gravy flavors are married, you can remove some into a separate pot so it can be cooled to go in the freezer.

Painting & Purpose

There's something very sacred about who a black woman chooses to remove their hair extensions. It's trust, first of all, because every black woman fears someone cutting their real hair during the take-down process of a protective hairstyle (braids, sew-ins, crochet hairstyles, or twists). My oldest daughter, Heaven, takes my hair down for me. She will grease my scalp every time I wash it as well. It's a certain type of love we have for each other. She saw me grow into who I've become, and often she'll say, "They don't know, but I know where you came from and how you got here." She saw the work, respected it, and gave it space when she knew it was time for things to flow a certain way.

I remember when I first painted artwork all over the walls of my old apartment. Those paintings were like therapy. It healed me in many ways to express myself in that way. I was often afraid that Heaven would think I was weird or an embarrassment, partially from me being a single mom when all of her friends had dads and two-parent households, and also partially from my art. My art was surrounding her. She'd wake up and see mannequin heads on the walls or paintings on the ceiling. One day I was lying down on the floor and looking up at the painting on the living room ceiling, listening to the song I had on repeat ("Bennie and the Jets") when I was painting it. She came in and laid down with me. We were talking about school, and to console her I said, "Heaven, you're so much better than me, you'll be fine. I was bad in school; you're nothing like me." She replied, and I'll never forget this moment: "Ma, you weren't bad, you just didn't have this," and waved her hands toward the painted walls. She didn't know it, but that was the first step to me

building a good self-esteem. Heaven is so great, she forced me to believe I was that great, because I knew that she came from and learned from me. If it wasn't for her, I wouldn't have kept up this whole fight. It's so hard to be yourself when you feel alone a lot. But I've seen the misery of conforming, and I'd never want my kids to pick blending in because it's easier and more acceptable. So that meant I had to allow my wings to spread and fly and distribute all of my gifts in order to deal with the pains of it all, so I could learn, so I could harvest lessons to help them on their path. She's my A-1 since Day-1, and I trust her with everything.

CRAWFISH BISQUE

6 TO 8 SERVINGS

This is a meal that's only made on a special occasion. My mama is allergic to crawfish, so this was a meal that my daddy would do because he loves it so much. I swear the best part is getting the filling out of the crawfish head after it's been swimming in the gravy. We clean out the head of the crawfish, stuff it with meat, and then soak the head in gravy. This bisque is an oldie but goodie, passed down through several generations of New Orleans cooks. It's a heavy lift in a way because of the steps, so if you get offered a plate, cherish it. And if you're somehow allowed to fix your own plate, don't hog the heads or you could end up with yours on a platter.

3 pounds crawfish tails, reserving about 25 of the heads
12 to 15 cups water
2½ cup chopped onions
1¼ cup chopped celery
1¼ cup chopped bell peppers
3 bundles green onions, chopped
3 tablespoons garlic
½ teaspoon crab, shrimp, and crawfish boil (liquid concentrate)
3 eggs, beaten
2 cups bread crumbs
2 cups flour
2 cups butter
Cajun seasoning
Piping bag
Cooked rice

1 Peel the crawfish (*do not throw away the shells*). Place the tail meat in a bowl. To prep the heads: Hold the crawfish head with one hand with the smooth side of the shell touching your palm. Place your pointer finger inside the crawfish head and with your thumb touching the legs, gently pull downward. You'll see that this makes it easier for you to remove everything from the insides of the head. Place the empty heads on the side for later. Separate the shells from the tail and remove the claws. Place the shells and claws in a large pot.

2 Add the water to the pot of shells and claws. Bring to a boil, then allow to simmer for 30 minutes. Strain the shells out of the water and set the stock aside.

3 Preheat the oven to 350°F.

4 Sauté the trinity (onions, celery, and bell peppers) and green onions in a large pan for 8 minutes over medium-high heat until they're nice and soft. Remove 1 cup of the trinity mixture and set aside for the gravy. Add the crab, shrimp, and crawfish boil to the pan. Add the tail meat and trinity mixture to a food processor and pulsate until it becomes close to a paste. Add the beaten eggs and bread crumbs to the processor. Mix well. Pipe the stuffing into the heads and bake on a large lined cookie sheet for 15 minutes.

5 Prepare the butter roux by melting the butter over medium-high heat. Once it's really hot, add the flour and whisk constantly until it begins to color. It will go from white to peanut butter brown. It takes a while, so relax and be patient. Once the roux is a peanut butter color, add the trinity, stock, green onions, garlic, and Cajun seasoning, to taste. Add the heads and simmer on low for 25 minutes.

6 Add the crawfish tails and top off with extra seasoning if you need it and serve over rice!

TIP: If you need help with making the roux, I have a tutorial available on YouTube: Cooking with Toya Boudy.

SWEET POTATO BISQUE

6 TO 8 SERVINGS

Everyone needs an impressive soup under their belt, and nothing says, "I'm about to impress the hell out of my guests" better than a good bisque. In some cities they call it chowder, but in New Orleans, when we make a thick, super-rich, creamy, full-of-flavor soup, we call it bisque. It can go either way, appetizer or entrée! It's all about how you put it together. This recipe is a clear example of bisque as an entrée. I love to make a meal feel like a production on a plate, and the hash does that by adding serious flavor and more texture. Partner it with good hot bread and a salad and honey you are sa-tis-fied. As an appetizer, I suggest serving it in small mugs. You can substitute the chicken stock for veggie stock, plant butter for regular butter, and nondairy milks for the heavy cream. Honestly, I feel like this would be a new contender on the family "must haves" list for Thanksgiving! The bisque is subtle but gives off a full savory sweet potato flavor and the hash is a delightful complement of texture and bright colors. Trust me, you probably won't have any leftovers, which is a big A+ for the cook!

FOR THE HASH

1 pound sweet potatoes, chopped into chunky pieces (see Tips)
3 tablespoons extra virgin olive oil
Salt and pepper
2 tablespoons butter
2 tablespoons chopped onion
2 tablespoons chopped green onion

1 (15-ounce) can corn, drained
2 tablespoons chopped cilantro

FOR THE BISQUE

1 white onion, chopped
1 bundle of green onions, chopped
3 to 4 garlic cloves, chopped
2 pounds sweet potatoes, chopped into chunky pieces

4 tablespoons (½ stick) salted butter
4 cups chicken stock
7 cups heavy cream
1 teaspoon smoked paprika
All-purpose seasoning (a garlic and herb blend will work)
Salt and pepper to taste

TO MAKE THE HASH

1 Preheat the oven to 425°F. Coat the sweet potatoes with the oil and season with salt and pepper. Bake for 30 minutes.

2 Add the butter.

3 In a large skillet over medium-high heat, sauté the onions, green onions, and corn for 8 to 10 minutes.

4 Add the cooked sweet potatoes to the pan and begin to gently toss until well incorporated, about 2 minutes. Set aside.

TO MAKE THE BISQUE

1 Sauté the onions, green onions, and garlic in a medium pot over medium-high heat for 7 minutes with a tablespoon of butter, until they're a nice caramelized color.

2 Add the 2 pounds of sweet potatoes and stock. Let this simmer uncovered for 10 minutes, until the potatoes are nice and soft.

3 Add the heavy cream, then emulsify or transfer it all to a food processor and process until it is a really creamy souplike texture (see Tips). This process should take 10 to 15 minutes.

4 Season it to taste with the smoked paprika, salt, and pepper.

———

TIPS: Begin with prepping the sweet potatoes for the hash so it can be done when you're finishing up with the bisque.

You're looking for a smooth and creamy kind of feel for the soup. But it's also up to you if you want it to be chunky.

POTATO SALAD

6 TO 8 SERVINGS

Rarely will you get a fish plate in New Orleans without macaroni and cheese, potato salad, and a slice of 7Up cake. The vegetable is always the cook's pick, but you can bet money that the rest will be there. Growing up, I wasn't a big fan of eating potato salad unless I was sitting at the counter watching my mama make it while the potatoes were still steaming. Nothing was like that first warm spoon. As I grew up it started to be one of the things that became a highlight on a plate, and one of the measuring sticks I used to help me judge if the plate was gonna be good. As soon as I get a plate in my hands, I take a taste of the potato salad. If it's good, then I know the plate is rolling! *In New Orleans, "rolling" means really good! The potato salad can be the measuring stick because so much effort is normally put behind the entrée and sometimes not enough attention is given to the sides, thinking the eater will be distracted by the main squeeze. But really good cooks make sure that every part of the plate is well seasoned and catered to. So if you open the plate and the potato salad is rolling, it's a sign that they cared about the smallest part of the plate, and this tells you the entrée will be a treat! You see how serious it is? It's not* just *food, it's a part of who we are!*

3 pounds potatoes, russet or new potatoes
1 teaspoon salt, more for the dressing
1 cup mayonnaise
¼ cup yellow mustard
⅓ cup dill pickle relish
3 large eggs, hard boiled
½ teaspoon smoked paprika
Pepper

1 Clean and peel the potatoes and add to a large pot. Cover with water and heat over medium heat to a boil. Sprinkle in about 1 teaspoon of salt.

2 Cook the potatoes until they are fork tender, 15 to 20 minutes.

3 Drain the potatoes and rinse under cold water. Add the potatoes back into the empty pot and place back on the stove top to cool slightly. Then mash with a large fork, making sure you don't mash completely, as you want them to be chunky.

4 In a small bowl, combine the ingredients for the dressing: mayonnaise, mustard, relish, salt, and pepper to taste.

5 Chop the hard-boiled eggs and add to the pot with the potatoes.

6 Spoon the dressing over the potatoes and gently stir to mix and coat the potatoes in the dressing. Place into a large bowl.

7 Cover and chill for at least 2 hours before serving.

CORN BREAD & BLACK BEAN SALSA

6 TO 8 SERVINGS

I remember one day in culinary school like it was yesterday. The class assignment included corn bread on the list of things to make. Chef Ruth was giving instructions and reminding us of other tasks to be completed and what we'd be graded on. Everyone walked off into the kitchen, and I turned to Chef Margaret and asked her if I could try out this idea I had, which would mean I was going away from the initial instructions given. She leaned in to whisper, "Do it." When I was done, I brought it to both of my professors, Chef Margaret grinning and Chef Ruth gazing at me with a look I knew well from my mama. It was a "You didn't follow the rules, but good job." I know what she was trying to do. She wanted me to respect principles and rules, and if I went outside the box, the results had to be above the mark. If you prefer, you can serve with tortilla chips instead of corn bread.

FOR THE CORN BREAD

1 cup all-purpose flour
1 cup yellow cornmeal
2/3 cup white sugar
1 teaspoon salt
3 1/2 teaspoons baking powder
1 egg
1 cup milk
1/3 cup vegetable oil
1 1/2 cups canned corn (well drained

TO MAKE THE CORN BREAD

1 Preheat the oven to 400°F.

2 Line a loaf pan with foil. Lining the pan with foil will help cleanup.

3 In a large bowl, combine the flour, cornmeal, sugar, salt, and baking powder.

4 Stir in the egg, milk, and vegetable oil until well combined.

5 Fold in the corn.

6 Pour the batter into the prepared pan.

7 Bake for 20 to 25 minutes, until a toothpick inserted into the center of the loaf comes out clean.

CONTINUES

FOR THE BLACK BEAN SALSA

1 (14-ounce) can corn, drained
1 (14-ounce) can black beans
3 cups sliced cherry tomatoes
½ red onion, diced
⅓ cup chopped cilantro
Juice from 1 freshly squeezed
 lime
1 teaspoon olive oil
1 teaspoon rice wine vinegar
2 avocados, diced
Salt and pepper

TO MAKE THE BLACK BEAN SALSA

1 Drain the corn and black beans.

2 Add all the ingredients except the avocado and salt and pepper together in a bowl. Mix well; add the avocados and salt and pepper to taste.

3 Serve with the hot corn bread.

LEMON PEPPER GREEN BEANS

4 TO 6 SERVINGS

Growing up, I only had green beans two ways. One was a side in grade school, which was bland. (Generally, I liked green vegetables, and so I ate them even if I felt they needed more flavor.) The other way was green beans smothered with potatoes and put over rice. In school, I was introduced to different styles of food than what we had at home. Styles where it wasn't about stretching it, but was about highlighting the goodness of the natural flavor. There was this lemon butter green beans recipe in one of my culinary classes in college, of all places. I looked it over when I first heard the name, but when I tasted it I thought, "Lemon and butter . . . what?! This is so good!" Until then, my favorite way to eat green beans had been smothered. Now, lemon pepper green beans is a go-to side for any protein for me, or I can eat a plate full of just these green beans.

1½ pounds green beans, stem ends trimmed

3 tablespoons butter

2 garlic cloves, minced

Juice of ½ large lemon

2 teaspoons black pepper

1 teaspoon salt

¼ cup finely grated Parmesan cheese

1 Bring a large pot of water to a boil. Add the trimmed green beans and cook for 3 minutes over medium-high heat.

2 While the beans are cooking, prepare an ice bath by adding ice to a large bowl (fill bowl halfway with ice) and add cool water so the bowl is filled about three-quarters of the way.

3 When the green beans are ready, drain them and add them to the ice bath. This will stop the green beans from cooking further and lock in the bright green color. When the green beans are cool to the touch, drain them from the ice bath and set aside.

4 In a large sauté pan, melt the butter over medium-low heat. When the butter is completely melted, add the minced garlic and sauté until fragrant, about 5 minutes. Next, add the lemon juice, salt, and black pepper.

5 Add the cooled green beans to the lemon pepper butter sauce. Stir until heated completely and well coated.

6 Add the Parmesan cheese to the green beans before serving.

CAJUN SMOTHERED POTATOES

SERVES 4

Smothered potatoes always had a place in the Sunday dinner rotation. It's definitely solid proof that we can smother anything in New Orleans, even a vegetable! This is one of the most flavorful potato sides I know; it's the most comforting way to eat them. I love all dishes with potatoes but this one is at the top of the list!

½ cup (1 stick) butter

2 tablespoons chopped garlic

1 pound andouille sausage, chopped

1 cup heavy cream

2½ to 4½ cups chicken stock

6 potatoes, quartered and cut into slices

Cajun seasoning

1 Melt the butter in a large skillet over medium-high heat. Sauté the garlic and andouille until caramelized and fragrant, about 8 minutes.

2 Add the cream, 2½ cups stock, and potatoes and simmer for 10 minutes, until fork tender. If you notice the stock reducing quickly before the potatoes are tender, add more stock a cup at a time until they are tender.

3 After the potatoes are tender, you can add the Cajun seasoning to taste. Once your desired flavor is achieved, remove from the heat and serve.

TOYA'S JOURNEY

HOLIDAYS AT HOME

I finally accepted that my career was shifting.

I'm not going to lie, that acceptance came long after Chris gave me some valuable advice as a manager and a friend. Chris said, "You have to stop allowing yourself to be so accessible to people who could possibly want to use you in some way." He was right: I had this thing with guilt when it came to helping people. I felt because I got out of the predicaments I was in, and made so many positive changes that people were often struggling to make, that I owed them solutions to their problems. I was tired of being drained by my lack of boundaries with others, especially when it came to dealing with stuff in my own house. Out of a craving to have a family-career balance, I created an essence in our home that was full of peace. All the while, I kept a reasonable level of transparency online. I know well that the world doesn't feel like the inside of the home, and that we can't count on the world to celebrate our wins and moments. And that's fine. At home we do a lot of celebrating of any milestones or accomplishments of any sort. Most times it's just us in the home, but I do a full spread of food and I even decorate for just about anything. I gained a different perspective of home from traveling.

At the airport, I noticed that I wouldn't be on the plane yet and I'd be scrolling through my family's photos. And this is just with me traveling quarterly. So what will happen when things speed up? Chris and I started preparing for that by spending a lot of time together, budgeting outings and in-home events, like our indoor skate nights that we hold in the house. Disco lights and LED lighting gear with takeout makes for a great memory of a night.

Back when I was studying culinary shows, I studied the actors, artists, and speakers—basically anyone who had a career and personal life balance I admired. I noticed that they all had a few key things in common: strategic decision-making, balance, and boundaries. I noticed that these people didn't accept any role or opportunity given to them just because it was there to be taken, and that they had a private world that was theirs outside of who they were in the public world. I had to learn to save a significant portion of my gift for my family to avoid being tapped out once I get home. We've created a vibe at home that makes me eager to return, and I feel like that's one of my greatest accomplishments. Our home is our safe space.

STUFFED PEPPERS

5 SERVINGS

You can maybe skip stuffed bell peppers for Thanksgiving, but you absolutely cannot skip having them for Christmas. All I think about is my mama heading to the store to catch the peppers on sale for the holidays, getting home, prepping them, and seeing the countertop filled with pans with peppers cut in half. I swear it felt like there was a sea of them. Every year it sparked a thought: "Who's going to eat all of these?" Us, that's who! Trust me, I remembered why she made so many once they were done and the kitchen lights cut off at night. That was my signal to sneak into the kitchen to put three bell pepper halves on a plate as a midnight snack. My mama has this way of making the stuffing just right. Not too much breading, never too many chopped veggies, so that they only focused on the full flavor that hit you from cheek to cheek. It was edible joy, and that's what it was: joy.

Even though we visit parents for the holiday and we're out a great deal of the day, I make a mini dinner for our own house and stuffed bell peppers are on the list. At the end of the night on Christmas we sort out toys, what needs batteries and what needs to be put together, and even though we ate the same food lineup during the day, there is something about being home and fixing Chris a plate while the kids play that brings me joy.

5 large bell peppers, any color, even in size, plus 1 bell pepper, chopped

1 onion, chopped

1 celery stalk, chopped

2 tablespoons bruised chopped garlic

1 pound ground breakfast sausage (Jimmy Dean is a local favorite for stuffing)

1 pound ground beef

5 tablespoons Cajun seasoning

1½ cups chicken stock

½ cup Italian bread crumbs

8 ounces lump crabmeat

Panko for sprinkling

Parsley for topping

1 Preheat the oven to 375°F.

2 Cut the bell peppers in half lengthwise, remove all the seeds, and scoop out the insides to make it smooth for filling. Line them up on a foil-lined baking pan and set aside.

3 In a large skillet over medium heat, sauté the onions, chopped bell peppers, celery, and garlic for about 8 minutes, until caramelized and fragrant.

4 Add the breakfast sausage to the pan to brown, about 12 minutes. Once browned, add that to a bowl and set aside.

5 Season the ground beef with 3 tablespoons of the Cajun seasoning before browning (if you brown ground meat without seasoning it first, it will let off a loud smell and lock in a bland taste). Brown the same way you did the breakfast sausage. Once the meat is browned, add the ground meat to the same bowl that contains the sausage and veggies. Mix them together well with a large spoon.

6 If you like your meat smooth rather than chunky, process it briefly in a food processor. The goal is to loosen it up slightly, so if you have a larger food processor, pulsing it twice will be enough. Again, the goal is not to make it a paste; you just want to loosen it up to make it even in texture. When done it should look like medium-fine ground meat.

7 Transfer everything back into the bowl. Add the chicken stock, the remaining Cajun seasoning, and bread crumbs. Mix well, then fold in the crabmeat.

8 Stuff the peppers until there's no empty spaces. Top with panko and parsley.

9 Bake for 25 minutes at 375°F and allow to rest for 10 minutes before serving.

CHRISTMAS CHICKEN

4 TO 6 SERVINGS

Though the cooking starts well before the "Big Day," you better not touch anything before December 25th! My mother would always cook a "shits and giggles" meal the day or two before just to silence the hunger that the delicious smells piqued. She would make a chicken dish of some sort. Something quick, baked, and easily paired with a simple side of hot rice or veggies. This Christmas chicken is the perfect fit for that type of meal. Crispy seared chicken thighs with drippings from the chicken are blended with sautéed cranberries and herbs to create a sophisticated feel on the palate and a merry joy to the eyes. The traditional red and green color combo serves as a flavorful garnish. Best served with hot, lightly salted rice or veggies of choice with some of the drippings and cranberries.

6 boneless chicken thighs
1 tablespoon coarse salt
1 tablespoon cracked pepper
3 tablespoons extra virgin oil
2 tablespoons minced garlic
2 tablespoons salted butter
1 cup fresh cranberries
2 long sprigs fresh thyme
1 teaspoon lemon juice

1 Season the chicken thighs with salt and pepper on both sides.

2 Add the oil and garlic to a large pan over medium heat and allow the thighs to get a good sear; it'll take 5 minutes.

3 Flip the thighs and add the butter, cranberries, thyme, and lemon juice. Cook for 8 minutes on both sides until the juices from the chicken run clear.

4 Serve piping hot!

DRESSING 4 WAYS

SERVES 6 TO 8

In New Orleans, dressing is a big thing. It's actually rare to find a stuffed turkey in a black household in New Orleans, and Thanksgiving isn't the only time we eat dressing. You can be judged from the start with the bread base: do you use Jiffy corn bread? Or that Mighty Martha White? Moving on to the meats, you can hear elders asking, "That's Jimmy Dean?" "You use gizzards?" One could hear those and think they're general questions, but to a cook in New Orleans, those answers will let people know if they have to wait until they get home to eat because it may not have the right flavor.

On a holiday, you can house-hop and get different dressings at each house because everyone has their own way, own feel and flavor. There's a difference between dressing for Christmas and Thanksgiving in most households. Growing up we had oyster dressing for Christmas and seafood for Thanksgiving. But trust and believe that either holiday will have a plethora of options and full flavors.

Don't get me wrong, we do "stuff" some things but it's not the same as you'd see from a different city. We're big on sides, and tons of options in general, for gatherings. Now for "dinners" (one unified meal served to a group) or restaurant experiences, you'll see "stuffed shrimp, chicken, or fish." There are also the times when you find that the main protein is "topped" or on top of a bed of dressing. It's safe to say we dance lightly around stuffing unless it's boudin sausage or a Snowball, the New Orleans version of shaved ice that can be stuffed with ice cream.

ORIGINAL DRESSING BASE

¼ cup (½ stick) butter

2 onions, chopped

1 bell pepper, chopped

1 celery stalk, chopped

1 bundle green onions, chopped

1 tablespoon chopped garlic

1 (16-ounce) pack Jimmy Dean sausage

1 (16-ounce) bag cubed toasted bread or 16 ounces baked corn bread or prepackaged stuffing

3 cups stock made with chicken bouillon (for a stronger chicken flavor)

1 Preheat the oven to 400°F.

2 Melt the butter in a saucepan and sauté onions, green onions, bell pepper, and celery until tender and caramelized. Set aside.

3 Brown the sausage, break it apart, and don't worry about the chunks.

4 Using a food processor or a blender, add meat and pulse a couple of times to break down the meat so it can be evenly distributed throughout the stuffing

5 In a large bowl, mix everything together until well combined.

6 Add to a baking dish, top with bread crumbs and parsley, and bake until golden.

7 Let set for 10 minutes before serving.

EGGPLANT DRESSING

1 medium eggplant
Oil
¼ cup (½ stick) butter
2 onions, peeled and chopped
1 bell pepper, destemmed, deseeded, chopped roughly
1 celery stalk, finely chopped
1 tablespoon garlic
1 (16-ounce) package breakfast sausage (I use Jimmy Dean)
2 to 3 cups stock (chicken or vegetable)
2 cups crumbled corn bread (I make an 8-by-8 pan from a 6.5-ounce Martha White corn bread mix, or store-bought)
Cajun seasoning

1 Prepare corn bread as the package directs and set aside.

2 Preheat the oven to 400°F. Line a 13-by-9-inch pan with foil.

3 Cut the eggplant in half and rub each half with a little oil on a foil-lined sheet. Bake them open side up for 15 minutes until the center is tender.

4 Remove the eggplant from the oven and scoop out the center, place it in a bowl, and set aside. You can discard the outer shells.

5 Melt the butter in a large skillet, and sauté the onions, bell peppers, celery, and garlic for 8 minutes, until tender and caramelized. Set aside on a plate and wipe out the pan.

6 In the same pan, brown the sausage, about 10 minutes, breaking it apart; don't worry about the chunks.

7 Using a food processor or a blender, pulse the meat a couple of times to break it down evenly in small pieces. Do this same thing with the eggplant; pulse it a few times until almost smooth.

8 In a large bowl, combine the eggplant, meat, and cooked vegetables. Toss thoroughly with your hands or a spoon. Add the stock slowly, starting with 2 cups. You want the mixture to be moist but not wet. Remember, it will dry out a bit when you bake it, so don't skimp on the stock. Season to taste, scrape into a nonstick 13-by-9-inch baking dish, and bake for 20 minutes, or until the top has risen slightly and feels dry. Let it set for 10 minutes, then serve.

CRAB AND CRAWFISH DRESSING

4 cups corn bread
¼ cup (½ stick) butter
2 onions, chopped
1 bundle of green onions,
    chopped
1 bell pepper, chopped
1 celery stalk, chopped
1 tablespoon garlic
1 (16-ounce) package Jimmy
    Dean sausage
2 pounds precooked crawfish
    tails with fat included
    (orange-colored liquid that
    comes with it in the package)
6 ounces precooked crabmeat
½ teaspoon crab, shrimp, and
    crawfish boil
3 cups stock (chicken or
    vegetable)
Cajun seasoning
Bread crumbs for topping
Parsley for topping

1 Prepare the corn bread as the package directs; once it's done, crumble it all and set aside.

2 Preheat the oven to 400°F.

3 Melt the butter in a large saucepan and sauté the onions, green onions, bell pepper, celery, and garlic for 8 minutes, until tender and caramelized. Set aside.

4 Brown the sausage, breaking it apart. Don't worry about the chunks.

5 Using a food processor or a blender, add the sausage and pulse a couple of times to break it down so it can be even throughout the stuffing.

6 In a large bowl, combine all the ingredients except the bread crumbs and parsley. Keep in mind that the crawfish and crab are precooked (they can't come out of their shells without being steamed first), so don't worry about sautéeing the seafood.

7 Once it's all mixed, add more Cajun seasoning to taste, pour in a baking dish, top with bread crumbs and parsley, and bake for 25 minutes until the top is golden. Let it set for 15 minutes, then serve.

OYSTER DRESSING

1 (16-ounce) box of corn bread

¼ cup (½ half stick) plus
    1 tablespoon butter

2 onions, chopped

1 bundle of green onions,
    chopped

1 bell pepper, chopped

1 celery stalk, chopped

1 (16-ounce) package Jimmy
    Dean sausage

1 tablespoon minced garlic

1 (16- to 20-ounce) jar of
    oysters, rinsed

2 cups shredded Parmesan
    cheese

3 cups stock (chicken or
    vegetable)

Cajun seasoning

Bread crumbs for topping

Parsley for topping

1 Prepare the corn bread as the package directs. Once it's done, crumble it all and set aside.

2 Preheat the oven to 400°F.

3 Melt the ¼ cup of butter in a large saucepan and sauté the onions, green onions, bell pepper, and celery for 8 minutes, until tender and caramelized. Set aside.

4 Brown the sausage for 10 minutes, breaking it apart. Don't worry about the chunks.

5 Add 1 tablespoon of the butter, garlic, and oysters to a small skillet and sauté for 5 minutes until fragrant and set aside.

6 Using a food processor or a blender, add the sausage and pulse a couple of times to break it down so it can be even throughout the stuffing. Remove the meat and do the same with the oysters, or you can just chop them up finely. Whichever you prefer.

7 In a large bowl, mix all the ingredients together except the bread crumbs and parsley, seasoning it with Cajun seasoning to taste. Top with bread crumbs and parsley and bake for 25 minutes until golden.

8 Let it set for 15 minutes, then serve.

BOURBON BROWN SUGAR SPIRAL HAM

8 TO 10 SERVINGS

Ain't nothing like a showstopping dish that's quick to make! I love brown sugar bourbon but ain't nothing like your own sauce. You can make it boozy and delicious! I always like to stretch it damn near to a salty savory dessert.

I love my holiday spread to have a mix of both easy and time-consuming dishes, just to give a little balance for me and my sanity. There's never a time I don't want ham during the holidays. My daddy broke everything down at the end of the holiday. He'd break the turkey down by carving it, preserving the drippings and putting them in a container. He did the same with gumbo, ham, or any meal that used a large pot or baking pan. I always loved when my daddy did the ham, because he'd snack on it while putting it in the container, and that allowed me to get more ham in one serving than I normally would: He'd taste a piece and say, "Aw, man, this shit is good! Taste it." Of course, we all knew what it tasted like already, but he's just the kind of person to feed you on the spot. Because he was enjoying, he felt you should too! He's cool like that, and also his ham is good as hell.

1 cup (2 sticks) unsalted butter

2 cups dark brown sugar

¾ cup bourbon

6- to 9-pound spiral ham

1 Preheat the oven to 350°F.

2 In a large saucepan, melt the butter. Add the brown sugar and cook over medium heat until the sugar is dissolved. Add the bourbon and mix well.

3 Place your ham in an oven-safe baking dish and cover it with half of the glaze mix. Make sure to reserve the rest of the glaze for later.

4 Bake the ham for 1½ to 2 hours until the internal temperature of the ham reaches 140°F with an instant read thermometer.

5 Pour the reserved glaze carefully over the ham.

6 Turn the oven to broil and broil the ham for about 5 minutes or so just to get it bubbly and pretty.

BLACK-EYED PEAS & COLLARD GREENS

6 TO 8 SERVINGS

I have memories scattered all over my childhood connected to New Year's Day and black-eyed peas. All delicious and fond memories. My parents worked to clean the greens and prep the black-eyed peas. My daddy would fry the corn bread patties to keep the rest of the meal company. For years I thought this was just a New Orleans tradition, but then I learned that all over the South, Southerners start off the year with this delicious combination, and each part has a special meaning. Collard greens symbolize money and a prosperous new year. With its origins stemming from Africa, the tradition for black-eyed peas is to bring luck and prosperity. Pork is added because the pig nudges its nose forward, and you want to move forward this year. So much more than a tasty meal, it's symbolic for the year to come. Setting intentions from the plate to the belly!

I wanted to offer an elevated version of that meal. The buttery feel of the fried black-eyed peas with a smoky taste, the flavor-packed collards with a light crisp at the end of the bite, the smooth, light, and salty coppa, and the hot honey corn bread with a sweet fresh tomato side (that I added because red is a lucky color in the Chinese culture) brings it at a high standard. Close your eyes with your first bite and enjoy thinking of the symbolism and what it means to you to have another year. Happy New Year and happy cooking!

FOR THE VINAIGRETTE

1 cup olive oil

2 tablespoons white vinegar

1 hearty tablespoon dill paste, (store-bought or homemade, see Tips), more if needed

1 hearty tablespoon mayo (if you don't want a creamy vinaigrette, leave out the mayo)

1 teaspoon garlic and herb seasoning (but honestly any seasoning blend you like will work), more if needed

FOR THE PEAS AND GREENS

4 (14-ounce) cans black-eyed peas

8 tablespoons (1 stick) butter

1 onion, chopped

1 bundle of green onions, chopped

1 to 2 tablespoons smoked paprika

2 teaspoons garlic paste or chopped garlic

1 teaspoon all-in-one seasoning blend, more if needed

1 (16-ounce) container Guidry's Creole seasoning

1 bag of triple-washed collard greens

2 tablespoons lime juice (optional)

6- to 12-ounce container of Sangria cherry tomatoes, sliced in half

3 ounces prosciutto or coppa slices

Corn bread, prepared from a mix (I like Krusteaz Honey Cornbread) or cornbread patties, made from frying the prepared batter like pancakes

TO MAKE THE VINAIGRETTE

Mix all the ingredients well; adjust taste to personal liking by adding more or less seasoning or dill paste. Set aside.

TO MAKE THE PEAS AND GREENS

1 Pour the cans of black-eyed peas in a colander, rinse off all the liquid to get rid of the "canned" taste. Allow to drain.

2 Melt 2 tablespoons of the butter in a large pan over medium-high heat, add the onions, green onions, garlic, and all-in-one seasoning, to taste. Sauté for 8 minutes until caramelized.

3 Add 2 tablespoons of the butter to the pan, add the black-eyed peas, and season to taste with seasoned salt if you need more, and add 1 to 2 tablespoons smoked paprika (gives the illusion of having a smoked meat flavor). Once seasoned to taste, set aside.

4 Melt 2 tablespoons of the butter in large pot or skillet over medium-high heat and sauté the Creole seasoning until tender. Add 2 more tablespoons butter and the collards and sauté for 15 to 25 minutes, until they begin to wilt slightly (see Tips). Begin to season to taste. Add the lime juice, if using, and remove from heat.

5 Toss the tomatoes with the vinaigrette. Top the collards with the prosciutto. Serve with the black-eyed peas and corn bread.

TIPS: Taste the collards as you go; you want to have some crunch.

To make your own dill paste, add 1 cup chopped fresh dill and 1 tablespoon olive oil to a food processor and blend well.

CONTINUES

Collard Greens

Greens were given to slaves as a part of their rations. But the benefits of collards warm my heart. Damn, even when they were trying to give us the least, somehow it worked in our favor. Out of all the pain and treacherous times that we took the scraps we were thrown, we made it gold.

Somehow, out of all that torture, we kept our souls, and trapped pieces of us within the flavor.

Glorious food after a hard day being our savior.

Turning pain into iconic meals that's traveled across states forcing everyone to acknowledge what was created. Collard greens were very popular among black people. But after the Civil War, white soldiers found themselves destitute, and collards became popular in the homes of soldiers as well. It's safe to say the Southern food world was built on our backs.

We've worked for seats that we don't need. Seats are bottom tier; baby we're the *table*.

ENDIVE APPETIZERS

SERVES 4

I'll be honest, I don't even know if these will make it to a party. I can eat the whole tray standing up, that's how good they are. Just a complete surprise of full flavor from the crunch of the endive to the herbed pecans, it's a complete TKO hands down. My firm suggestion is to make double! My mama was at the house the day I cooked this for the photo shoot. She saw the photo pop up after Sam took the shot and said, "Oh that's beautiful." *Sam interjected and said, "Oh, it's good!" I pushed her to try it, because she's not a fan of trying new things like goat cheese, but she* loved it! *She was surprised and I was pleased as well. It's so damn pretty too!*

3 large endives, leaves
    separated
1½ cups goat cheese
3 tablespoons prosecco wine
    vinegar
1 cup chopped pecans
2 tablespoons salted butter
1 teaspoon herbes de Provence
½ teaspoon salt

1 Line up the endive leaves on a serving tray or platter and set aside.

2 Add the goat cheese to a medium bowl and using a spoon, break the cheese into smaller crumbles. Toss with the vinegar and set aside.

3 Add the pecans, butter, salt, and herbs to a medium saucepan and sauté about 5 minutes, until toasty and fragrant. Remove from heat.

4 Now it's time to assemble! Spoon a teaspoon and a half of marinated goat cheese into each leaf and sprinkle with pecans. Finish the rotation until all the leaves are filled. Serve and enjoy.

PRALINE BACON

SERVES 6

Do you really need a reason? Seriously, salty, hickory, smoky bacon with woodsy pecans and sweet brown sugar stickiness? It's a firm yes for me! I first started making this for Valentine's Day. Every year I make a "Bacon, Berries, and Beignets with the Boudys" spread for breakfast for the whole house. Regular bacon, praline bacon, and turkey bacon with chocolate-covered berries along with beignets (page 123). Instantly these are gone from the table. So take the empty plate's word for it. You'll love it! Double or triple the recipe if you like.

1 (16-ounce) pack thick-cut hickory bacon
1 cup chopped pecans
1 cup brown sugar

1 Preheat the oven to 425°F.

2 Add a baking rack to a sheet pan to allow the bacon to cook elevated, allowing the fat to drip so the bacon can be drier versus swimming in the fat. We need the bacon to be separate from the fat so that the sugar can sit on top instead of the bacon fat washing it away.

3 Line up the bacon on the rack and bake for about 15 minutes, then sprinkle with the pecans and then the brown sugar.

4 Bake for 3 minutes. Check on it to see if the sugar is melting; if it needs help, spoon some of the bacon fat on the bacon, and bake for about 2 more minutes. Remove from the oven and allow to cool. It's absolutely delicious!

PRALINE SWEET POTATOES WITH WHISKEY MALLO CREAM

6 TO 8 SERVINGS

One of my biggest chants is "If ya ain't doing the most, ya doing the least." When I first made this dish, I said, "Toya this doesn't make any sense, why is this so good!" This is not your granny's sweet potatoes. The whiskey mallo cream is the perfect flex and show-off, creating a moment at the table that you didn't know you needed. Make it and bask in the glory of the wowing compliments!

5 sweet potatoes, peeled and cut into ¼-inch slices
½ cup (1 stick) unsalted butter
½ teaspoon cinnamon
½ teaspoon nutmeg, more for topping
1 cup light brown sugar
½ cup pecans
7 to 8 ounces marshmallow fluff
¼ cup whiskey, more if needed

1 Preheat the oven to 400°F. Line a 13-by-9-inch baking dish with foil sprayed with cooking spray. Line the sweet potatoes in the pan, slightly overlapping each other and set aside.

2 In a small saucepan, melt the butter, cinnamon, nutmeg, brown sugar, and pecans. Once melted and well mixed, pour the mixture over the sweet potatoes and cover with foil and bake for 20 minutes or until desired tenderness.

3 When the potatoes are almost done, add all the marshmallow fluff to a medium bowl along with the whiskey and whisk it with a hand mixer until it's loose. Not thin at all but can run off the spoon like super thick cream. Add a shot more of whiskey if you want it runny.

4 Add two tablespoons of the marshmallow to each plate, spoon on some sweet potatoes, and sprinkle it with nutmeg and serve.

BOURBON-GLAZED LAMB CHOPS WITH MARINATED BEANS

This is personal. Even the way I plate this has meaning. The triune (beginning, middle, and end): the splash of red paprika over the entire plate, the chops of lamb, and the beans all combine to symbolize the resurrection and reincarnation. It's meant to remind us of the cycle of life: giving, sacrifice, and resurrection. My first time having lamb was in a Middle Eastern café in New Orleans. The tenderness, taste, and freshness of that dish was perfect. I love beans done any way, but this style is actually the way I cook them if I'm meal-prepping for myself. When I first made this meal I did it with my daddy in mind. He's the one who inspired me to be adventurous with food, and he really believed you should embrace other cultures too. The touch of bourbon in the sauce was the only New Orleans flair I added to it. I wanted to respect the fond memory of my first encounter with lamb at that Middle Eastern café as much as possible. When my daddy tried it he called me and said, "Toy, this was perfect." My parents are the most rewarding people to cook for, because they're honest and they know good food. Truthfully, they were always my template for cooking, and they're a real inspiration to me. The beans could also be served with any other dish as an impressive side dish!

FOR THE LAMB CHOPS

12 (3-ounce) lamb loin chops
Truffle salt
Cracked pepper
About ½ cup salted butter
1 to 2 teaspoons minced garlic
¼ cup dark brown sugar
¼ cup bourbon
Marinated Beans, recipe follows

FOR THE MARINATED BEANS

2 tablespoons extra virgin olive oil
1 garlic clove, peeled and bruised
2 cans cannellini beans
1 teaspoon prosecco wine vinegar
1 teaspoon herbes de Provence
¼ teaspoon smoked paprika
¼ teaspoon salt, more if needed
¼ teaspoon pepper, more if needed

CONTINUES

TO MAKE THE LAMB CHOPS

1 Lightly season the chops with salt and cracked pepper on both sides.

2 Melt 1 to 2 tablespoons of the butter in a large skillet over medium-high heat. Sear the chops 3 minutes on each side or until cooked to your liking. Do this in batches if needed. Remove from the skillet and set aside.

3 Add ¼ cup of the butter, garlic, brown sugar, and bourbon to the skillet. Bring to a simmer over medium heat, then add the chops back into the skillet for a minute or two, making sure all the sides get coated. Set aside for serving.

TO MAKE THE MARINATED BEANS

1 Add the oil and garlic to a medium nonstick pan and sauté over medium heat for 5 minutes until fragrant.

2 Add the beans, vinegar, and all the remaining seasonings.

3 Simmer on a low temp for 10 minutes and adjust the taste with salt and pepper to your liking.

4 Serve and top with the lamp chops.

CHAPTER FIVE

SWEETS AND SIPS

Good food and trust

Teamwork makes the dream work.

Chris and I are together every step. Even if it's something I'm spearheading, he will always be near to protect me in every way.

When I asked him if he wanted to partner with me on a new project, he said, "You know how I am, logistics and answers, that's what I want. But with this new venture I don't have that at the moment. Toya, when you start the train to a new thing, I just look back at your track record and I punch my ticket." It's trust. We trust each other. So much so that on our honeymoon he booked an excursion in the Caribbean Sea and I couldn't swim! There I was, in the deepest water I've ever seen, with land far away, learning to swim. That's the nature of our relationship, personally and professionally. He taught me how to swim and I taught him how to leap, together each step of the way.

It's the sweet things that's etched in our memories that helps us through tough times in life. That's why when tough times come, sometimes something sweet and comforting—or even a good drink—will make a rocky moment mellow out. This chapter is a sweet ending to a portion of my journey through food and life lessons. It will always come back to the food. Good times or bad, wins or losses. Good food will forever be the life of the party.

COOKIES & CREAM ICE CREAM

6 SERVINGS

At the top of my first pregnancy, my sister Elise took me under her wing. Any time I wasn't at school I'd be by her house, especially on the weekends. At the time she was a nail tech and worked in a hair salon. In middle school I used to charge girls $10 to style their hair, so she knew I could earn some money helping around the salon. She asked the owner if I could work shampooing heads or doing the occasional roller set to prep the hair for the stylist on Saturdays. Doing that, I could make $25 a day. That money was enough to handle my weekly cravings for snacks from the concession stand at school just so I could make it through the day. Breakfast and lunch alone was never enough to cover my pregnancy eating habits. I had an idea that my first year of high school would be full of new experiences, but I definitely had not planned on spending that first year pregnant and smuggling snacks into class.

When I got off the bus, damn near every day I'd go straight to the store to get canned ravioli, which tastes bomb with a little Cajun seasoning, and cookies and cream ice cream. It was a tiny ritual that made me feel slightly normal, slightly free. I spent so much time at home in my room disappointed in myself, but there were moments of hope. Riding the school bus and walking home alone was the closest I got to feeling like an adult, especially when I made the choice to stop at the store and pull out my own cash, buying what I wanted. In that moment I felt like I could skip out of my current situation, which in my opinion felt like I was becoming a "fixer upper" project for my parents and siblings. This was all tough for my mama, and though it was hard on her to watch her baby having a baby, she embraced it. At times, she would even drive to get whatever I was craving. Like any New Orleanian knows, hard times come. And for all the things you can't control, sometimes food is the only thing that can be the silver lining. Those meals cradled me through these changing times. It felt like I stumbled upon golden nuggets when I would get big chunks of cookie in my ice cream instead of just the normal cookie crumble. I get a glance at my past when I'm walking down the aisle in the grocery store, thinking, "Twenty-two years ago, some days that cookies and cream ice cream was my highlight in a dark portion of my story." Man, oh man, I'm far away from those days, but I still look back and give a loving glance at me pushing through all of that thick sand to get here. Those days were heavy, but nothing was able to sink my ship. This recipe is rich in cream and it gives a take-your-shoes-off-to-enjoy-it kinda feel when you eat it. Definitely a top-tier comfort food.

CONTINUES

1 (15-ounce) package Double
  Stuf Oreos
4 cups heavy whipping cream
3½ cups sweetened condensed
  milk
1 teaspoon vanilla extract

1 Break up all the cookies into chunks, some big and some small and
  set them aside.

2 In a large bowl, whip the heavy cream until it has a thick and fluffy
  appearance (peaks).

3 Gently fold in the condensed milk, vanilla, and majority of the
  cookies until it's well mixed.

4 Pour the mixture into an airtight glass container and top with the
  remaining cookies, then freeze for 8 hours, or until it's firm. The
  easiest way is to freeze it overnight so you can wake up to a nice
  surprise!

5 Scoop and enjoy!

STRAWBERRY SHORTCAKE

SERVES 12

I worked at a hair salon and then at a local grocery store as a cashier. When putting groceries back at the end of my shift I'd talk to the workers in the other departments. There was this kind woman in the bakery, and I complimented her cakes and frosting. She said, "It's easy. You wanna know how to make it?" I quickly said, "Yes!" I walked behind the counter to watch, and it was "murder she wrote" after that! Anything I'd eat at work I'd try to duplicate at home when I could. One day I ate the strawberry shortcake, and years later I made it. My daughter Heaven loved it, and it became her birthday cake for a few years. Recently, when she turned 21, she asked for a version of it, and it melted my heart all over again.

FOR THE SHORTCAKE

1 cup full-fat sour cream
½ cup whole milk
2 teaspoons vanilla extract (can use clear extract)
½ teaspoon almond emulsion (optional)
1 teaspoon butter extract or emulsion (optional)
6 large egg whites
2½ cups all-purpose flour (or 2¾ cups cake flour, for an even whiter cake)
2 cups sugar
½ teaspoon baking soda
1½ teaspoons baking powder
1 teaspoon salt
⅔ cup shortening
¼ cup unsalted butter, cut into chunks (room temperature)

TO MAKE THE SHORTCAKE

1 Preheat the oven to 325°F.

2 Grease and flour two 8-inch round (2 inches deep) cake pans. You could also use three 6-inch round pans.

3 In a medium bowl, mix together the sour cream, milk, vanilla extract, almond emulsion (if using), butter extract (if using), and egg whites. Whisk until smooth and set aside.

4 In a large mixing bowl, add the flour, sugar, baking soda, baking powder, and salt. Whisk together.

5 Add the shortening and butter chunks to the flour mixture.

6 Mix until the flour is coated with the shortening and butter. The mixture will be crumbly.

7 Add in half of the sour cream mixture and mix just until combined.

8 Add in the last half of the sour cream mixture and mix just until combined.

9 Scrape down the sides of the bowl and then mix again, only for 10 to 15 seconds. You want to be careful not to overmix the batter.

10 Pour into the greased and floured cake pans and bake for 45 to 50 minutes, or until a toothpick comes out clean.

11 Cool on a wire rack, then begin frosting.

CONTINUES

FOR THE WHIPPED CREAM TOPPING

2 quarts heavy whipping cream
1 teaspoon vanilla
Up to 1 cup powdered sugar

FOR THE STRAWBERRY TOPPING

2 pints strawberries
¼ cup sugar
Mint for garnish (optional)
Melted chocolate for topping (optional)

TO MAKE THE WHIPPED CREAM TOPPING

1 In a large bowl or mixer, pour in the cream and vanilla and whip at a medium-high speed until it begins to peak and look like creamy clouds.

2 Add the powdered sugar, starting with a half cup. Whip it in, then taste it to see if you want to add the rest. Once you've reached the desired sweetness, you can cover and place it in the fridge until you're ready to use it.

TO MAKE THE STRAWBERRY TOPPING

1 Thoroughly clean the berries and remove the stems and slice them all up and place them into a container.

2 Add the sugar, stir around, and place the lid on and allow to sit in the fridge for 30 minutes. The sugar will combine with the natural juices and form strawberry magic.

TO SERVE

Option 1 On the first cake layer, spoon some of the whipped cream and top with strawberries, saving some for the top layer as well. Add the second layer and repeat. Serve and store in the fridge. This method will work well if you're sure that the cake will be consumed at the gathering so you wouldn't worry about the cake becoming soggy or wet from the berries.

Option 2 Top the cake by the slice: Cut a slice of cake and spoon the whipped cream and berries on as you serve it. Option 2 is the better choice for keeping the ingredients fresher tasting.

PUMPKIN ROLL

SERVES 12

I was no stranger in the kitchen. My parents acknowledged my skills but never "requested" anything, until this. It was Thanksgiving in 2000, and everyone knew I was practicing rolls, like jelly rolls and pumpkin rolls, and everyone fell in love with them. So this was my first addition to our Thanksgiving dinner, which is a big thing in black households, because if you mess something up, they'll rib the sleeves off of you (make fun of obnoxiously). Luckily, I had this on lock, and I did myself proud.

FOR THE SPONGE CAKE

¾ cup all-purpose flour
¼ teaspoon salt
1 teaspoon baking soda
1 teaspoon ground cinnamon
3 large eggs
1 cup granulated sugar
1 teaspoon vanilla extract
⅔ cup canned pumpkin

TO MAKE THE SPONGE CAKE

1 Preheat the oven to 350°F. Line a jelly roll pan (15-by-10 inches) with parchment paper, leaving an extra inch of parchment sticking up on both long sides of the pan so that you can easily lift the cake out after baking. (You can *very* lightly grease the parchment paper, if you want to, but you don't need to!)

2 In a large bowl, whisk together the flour, salt, baking soda, and cinnamon. In a separate large bowl, mix the eggs, sugar, vanilla, and pumpkin until smooth.

3 Add the dry ingredients to the bowl of wet ingredients and stir just until combined and no dry streaks remain.

4 Spread the batter evenly in the prepared pan.

5 Bake for 14 to 15 minutes, until a toothpick inserted in the center comes out clean.

6 Immediately lift the parchment paper and hot cake out of the pan and onto a flat (heat-safe) surface.

7 While the cake is hot, starting at one of the short ends, use your hands to gently and slowly roll the cake (and parchment paper!) all the way up. Allow it to cool completely on top of a wire cooling rack. (This allows it to cool underneath the roll and keeps the cake from sweating.)

CONTINUES

FOR THE FILLING

8 ounces softened cream cheese
2 tablespoons unsalted butter
1 teaspoon vanilla
1 cup powdered sugar, leave
    about 2 tablespoons
    reserved for dusting

TO MAKE THE FILLING

1   While the cake roll is cooling, mix the cream cheese, butter, vanilla, and powdered sugar together with an electric mixer until it is fluffy and smooth.

2   Once the cake roll is cooled completely, unroll it very carefully. Gently smooth the filling in an even layer over the cake.

3   Roll up the cake without the parchment paper. Cover with plastic wrap and refrigerate for at least 1 hour before serving.

4   Dust the top with powdered sugar, if desired. You could use a duster, spoon, or even your fingers to lightly sprinkle it on top of the roll. Cut into slices and serve.

7UP CAKE

SERVES 12

I was unique in many ways as a child, one of them being that I didn't like frosting on cakes. I always felt like cake was the true star and frosting often stole the show. My mama always made our birthday cakes and whenever it was time for my birthday, I would pick a 7Up cake or, interestingly enough, blueberry muffins. Wanna know what really wraps me around the pinkie of the 7Up cake? The crumbs . . . oh my word, it gets me every time with its crispy golden brown goodness. The only time we had soda in the house was when my mama would buy 7Up, which was just for her after a long day of work with her lunch or dinner (of course we did not play with my mama, so we never touched her soda), for a gathering of some sort, or if she was making this cake. This is my mama's recipe. I'm so honored. She baked it herself and brought it to the shoot. My mama was well aware of how I work, which is quick and intense. We shot over 70 recipes in 10 days, and she wanted to help me somehow, any way she could, even if it was keeping the kids so we could rest. What really topped it all off is that she gave me the recipe handwritten, and if you have parents who are older you know those are the things you hold tight to. Seeing our mama's handwriting makes me feel as if I have a frozen piece of time in my hands. That handwriting is what all of our New Orleans mothers have due to penmanship classes. I'll never forget Sam's (the food photographer) response to the cake. He was blown away by the texture, the flavor, and the lingering of its taste. My mama ain't no joke.

Baking spray
1½ cups butter (3 sticks)
3 cups sugar, sifted
5 eggs
3 cups cake flour, sifted (sifted
   after it's measured)
¾ cup 7Up
1 teaspoon vanilla extract
1 teaspoon butter extract
1 teaspoon almond extract

1   Preheat the oven to 350°F and spray a 10-inch Bundt pan with baking spray.

2   Cream the butter with a mixer until fluffy; it should take 2 minutes.

3   Add the sugar and continue to beat until it's well blended.

4   Add the eggs and blend until it's well incorporated.

5   Alternately add the flour and 7Up, add one half, mix well, and then repeat with the remaining portion. Add the extracts. We're using three different extracts because it builds an amazing flavor.

6   Scrape the batter into the Bundt pan. Smooth the top and tap to even out the batter.

7   Bake for 1 hour, or until a toothpick comes out clean. Let cool in pan.

PEACH COBBLER

SERVES 6

I love the old-school faves. Flavors that comfort and make you wanna take your shoes off, flavors that jog your memory of pleasant times and loved ones. My sister Emma makes the best peach cobbler, and what's interesting about that is she went to college in Atlanta and decided to live there, but when she would visit she would make a cobbler and that was the only time we had it because she made it so well. I thoroughly enjoyed it! I'm also that annoying person who will dig out more dumplings than peaches. I know, I know. How could I? The better question is shouldn't they have beat me to the cobbler? You'll understand better when you try it. Trust me.

8 ripe fresh peaches, peeled and sliced

2½ tablespoons cornstarch

About 2 cups granulated sugar

1 cup all-purpose flour

2 large eggs, yolks and whites separated

¼ cup butter, melted

1 teaspoon baking powder

2 large egg whites, beaten until stiff

1 Preheat the oven to 375°F.

2 Combine the peaches, cornstarch, and 1 cup sugar in a large bowl, then transfer to a greased 13-by-9-inch baking dish.

3 Wipe out the bowl and add the flour, egg yolks, butter, baking powder, and 1 cup sugar. Mix thoroughly.

4 Whip the 4 egg whites in a different large bowl until they just hold a peak. Gently fold the egg whites into the batter, keeping it light.

5 Spread the batter over the peaches (it might not cover every peach, but that's okay).

6 Bake until the peach mixture is bubbling around the edges and the top is golden, about 45 minutes.

WHITE CHOCOLATE BREAD PUDDING

SERVES 12

In New Orleans, you can go to multiple spots in the French Quarter to find white chocolate bread pudding on the menu because it's rich, fabulous, and everyone wants to eat it! New Orleans is known for this bread pudding, because of the French and Spanish upper class settlers who came here. Truth is, this dish started out in the lower class population, because it was made from leftover stale bread. Chefs in Europe took the recipe and refined it, and made it popular in Europe across all classes of people. Around 1880, new renditions of the recipe popped up in Creole cookbooks. It went from regular bread pudding, which was a standard style, sweetened with a milky eggy custard and baked into a bread-style casserole to a bread pudding with different fillings and sauces, from white chocolate to bourbon or rum. I'm a big texture person, so super-wet bread pudding wasn't on my to-do list. I tried it, and thought I wanted to find a happy medium for people who love bread pudding and for people who have texture issues and normally don't like it. I wanted my bread pudding to have the feel of molten chocolate cake. And so it does. My sister who doesn't normally like the texture of bread pudding loves mine, as well as my daddy who loves bread pudding even if it's wet.

FOR THE BREAD PUDDING

2 cups heavy cream
2 cups milk
2 cups white chocolate melting chips (13-ounce bag)
4 eggs
½ cup sugar
2 teaspoons vanilla
¼ teaspoon salt
6 to 8 cups French bread, torn into small cubes
1 tablespoon butter for buttering the pan

TO MAKE THE BREAD PUDDING

1 Preheat the oven at 350°F.

2 Over medium heat in a medium pot, heat the heavy cream with 1 cup of the milk.

3 Pour in the white chocolate chips and turn off the heat; let it sit and melt.

4 In a large bowl, whisk the eggs and set aside.

5 When the white chocolate mixture has cooled some, add the sugar, vanilla, salt, and remaining 1 cup cold milk. This will cool it down enough so the eggs won't scramble when they're added.

6 Slowly add this mixture to the egg mixture while whisking.

7 Once all the milk mixture is added, add the torn-up French bread to the bowl and let it soak for 15 to 20 minutes.

8 Butter a 13-by-9-inch pan and pour in the bread mixture.

CONTINUES

9   Bake for 60 to 70 minutes.

10 It will rise some in the oven simply because both bread and dairy swells. Don't worry. I like to cover it with foil and allow it to sit and deflate before serving.

FOR THE WHITE CHOCOLATE SAUCE

2½ cups heavy cream
8 ounces white chocolate, finely chopped
1 cup powdered sugar
Rum

TO MAKE THE WHITE CHOCOLATE SAUCE

1   Over medium heat in a medium pot, heat the heavy cream, add the white chocolate, and stir until melted, then remove it from the heat.

2   Add the powdered sugar and the rum to taste and stir to combine.

3   Drizzle over the entire bread pudding or spoon it on as you serve.

LAVENDER TEA CAKES

SERVES 6 TO 8

Tea cakes are one of my mama's favorites. It says a lot about her taste, because it's classic, with simple and nostalgic flavors. There is something wowing about simple recipes like this. It automatically makes me feel as if it was first created from a pure crave with the ingredients the bakers had around them. The sweet yet mild flavor of these cakes is perfect with a nice hot cup of tea. Adding lavender to the cake makes for a soothing bedtime nightcap that will help you to unwind and be mindful about your now.

4 to 5 cups self-rising flour
2 cups sugar
¼ teaspoon salt
2 eggs
½ cup oil
½ cup milk
1 teaspoon vanilla flavoring
1 teaspoon almond flavoring
1 teaspoon lavender extract
Lavender for garnish (optional)

1 Preheat the oven to 450°F.

2 Place the flour, sugar, and salt in a large mixing bowl.

3 Make a well in the center and add the remaining ingredients except the lavender garnish. Mix until all the ingredients are thoroughly combined. The dough will be stiff.

4 Place on a lightly floured surface and knead for 2 minutes. Roll out about 13 inches wide and cut using a cup.

5 Place on a baking stone and bake for 7 to 9 minutes, until lightly browned.

6 Garnish with lavender, if desired. Cool and enjoy.

HURRICANE

1 SERVING

In New Orleans, drinking is handled differently than in other cities. Most cities have last calls and days they don't sell liquor, but we don't have any of that. And we can actually walk around with drinks, and even go to a drive-thru to get any alcoholic beverages. Yep! Get a drink, and you can drive home to enjoy it! The hurricane is one of our signature drinks here, and just like everything it's coupled with a story. Well, during World War II whiskey was hard to come by, and that was a tough swallow for a city packed with bars. A restaurant owner made this drink in order to make use of the rum they had, and to boost sales. Traditionally, the drink came in a glass the shape of a hurricane lamp—an idea that was clever as hell! Like any hurricane, if you're not prepared it'll knock you on your ass! I'm more of a "make a drink in my own home" kind of person. I generally feel like some drinks served in public places are set up to make you need two. This is one of my favorite drinks to have after dinner. It's so grown. It's so good. And it's so New Orleans.

2 ounces white rum
2 ounces dark rum
2 ounces passion fruit juice
1 ounce orange juice
1 ounce lime juice
½ ounce simple syrup
½ ounce grenadine
Orange slices and maraschino
   cherries for garnish
   (optional)

1 Add ice and all the ingredients except the fruit into a cocktail shaker and shake well.

2 Strain into a glass and make sure to fill the glass with ice if it's warm out!

3 Garnish with an orange slice and cherry, if desired. I think it makes this drink so much prettier!

LEMONADE 4 WAYS

12 TO 16 SERVINGS

Honey, some days, months, weeks, or even years are so tough that you feel as sour as a lemon. At those times when life gives you lemons, make lemonade and spike it! This would be absolutely perfect for a brunch. You can make a large batch of the spiked lemonade using the original recipe and have other fruits ready to mix in as an option, or you can go ahead and choose a fruit and let its flavor be the star!

ORIGINAL LEMONADE

1 gallon water (16 cups)
3½ cups sugar
5 cups lemon juice (I strongly suggest buying organic lemon juice)
Chardonnay

1 Add the water to a large enough pitcher that can handle all the ingredients (2-gallon pitcher or serving bowl).

2 Add the sugar and lemon juice and mix until the sugar is dissolved. If you need it to be made quickly, warm water dissolves sugar super fast.

3 Add the chardonnay to taste.

CITRUS LEMONADE

1 lemon, chopped into small wedges
3 oranges, peeled and chopped

1 Mix together well and add to a serving bowl with a small spoon.

2 Spoon 2 tablespoons into the glass and mix or shake with a shaker with ice.

BLACKBERRY LEMONADE

1 pint blackberries
¼ cup sugar

1 Clean the berries, place them in a bowl, and smash some and leave some whole.

2 Add the sugar, mix well, and refrigerate for 30 minutes and place in a bowl for serving.

3 Add 2 to 3 tablespoons to each drink.

STRAWBERRY LEMONADE

4 cups chopped strawberries
¼ cup sugar
2 tablespoons lime juice
2 tablespoons lemon juice

1 Add all the ingredients together and let soak in the fridge for 30 minutes.

2 Add ¼ cup of the fruit mixture to each glass, mix well, and enjoy.

Final Thoughts

I walked into my own heart and said, "This is a holdup. Give me all of those words back that were spoken against you, it ain't *you*."

So much of what is criticized, called ghetto, or looked at as lacking class should really be praised. Braids, gold teeth, bold bright colors, dances from our motherland. Our hair that grows toward the sun, saluting the universe, is labeled as unruly or disruptive. Our speech that's heavily decorated with our swag and creative vernacular is received in a negative light. Tattoos that simply tell the stories about where we've been should be celebrated, the way Egyptians and African tribes had markings. Just to show a few examples.

I have moved into a new mental space of taking back the bad and making it good. I decided to stop the pain to consider what was really happening. I look back to an example like watermelon, and the mockery made of it in cartoons poking fun at the fruit that came from Africa, as if it were a shameful thing for black people to love watermelon. I tilted my head one day to view it from a different perspective. Watermelon is a majestic wonder, able to hydrate and feed with vitamins and nutrients. It's ability to grow in sandy soil shows how rich the soil and sand is in Africa.

Funny, the problem people have with you is really a problem they're having with themselves. That's heavy and that's real. From that point of realization on, I didn't "tuck" my accent or style anymore. My image and style reflects a flare and vibe that stems from my ancestors and the city I grew up in. So with every chance I get to represent our culture I do it. From my hair, head wraps, style, nails, or my diction, I wear it proudly and perform well, snatching back what has been said, and turning that negativity into inspiration to be unapologetically me. Just the way God created me to be.

"I'm the new age rags to riches story."

It was an interesting experience reliving a story that normally I'd just break down to a paragraph or two. Then to look back and see how I was protected or how others could have even felt witnessing me going through all of that. Looking back, I cheer on the younger version of me. "Keep going, Toya. Don't stop, Toya. It'll get better, Toya, trust what you believe and see in your mind. It will all come alive one day, I promise." I've found myself overwhelmed with joy and gratitude that I have the opportunity to share how I got to this place. I wrote a poem in 2012, and it had a line that said, "I'm the new age rags to riches story." It was crafty but it was true.

I never blamed anyone for thinking I wouldn't grow past my mistakes, because I know that it was a rough sight to see. It takes a skilled eye to know that a certain piece of coal could turn into a diamond after some heat and pressure. I was that coal that turned into the diamond, that rose that grew from concrete.

ACKNOWLEDGMENTS

There's no way I can start this without first acknowledging Ernest and Emily Thomas, my parents. You two said yes to God concerning my life when you said yes to each other. You two said yes to my life and who I'd become when you didn't give up on me. You helped me when I couldn't help myself, said multiple "no's" to yourselves to give us your best. One overflowing cup of being taught by actions, two cups of generosity, one cup and a half of tough love, and an overflowing cup of dedication produced three successful children, and I am so glad God gave us the two of you for our parents. I love you deeply. My sisters Emma and Elise, having you two in my corner to always support me has been a personal blessing to my career. You guys protect me and dream with me. I appreciate you both. To my beloved children, Heaven, Emmanuel, and Binah, thank you for sharing me with the world. I love and value the way you believe in me. I'm so grateful that I get to be your mother and you guys are my greatest gifts. Everything that I do is for you to have a bigger boost over the wall of success. I hope this book makes you proud.

To my forever professor Chef Ruth Varisco of Nunez Community College, I thank you for believing in me and coaching me through this journey. You never stopped teaching and guiding me. You'll be forever in my heart. Dr. Adam and Dr. Ava Richardson, you welcomed me when I was 16 and pregnant. When many looked down on me, you invested time into teaching me and guiding me to have a full relationship with God. You and your family will always have my love. I'm grateful for you.

To my team: Sam Hanna, thank you for cradling my vision as if it were your own. You took it all to heart and it showed. You are outrageously talented. My cousin, friend, and makeup artist Krystal Burrell, we dream together, believe together, and we create together. Thank you for living up to all of those titles brilliantly. David Richardson, you caught the frequency and helped birth the culture visuals, and you didn't miss—you were right on target every time. It was the execution I hoped for. Mariah Walton Bencik, just as a camera captures a moment, your eye for style can build one. The essence, look, and feel was assisted by your meticulous eye for detail. Sara Hudson, your support and nudging my way to this new place will forever be in my heart. Christopher Aramburo Boudy Sr., my co-captain, you run a ship so smooth I could put on mascara during a rocky storm. You do every single job as if it's for passion not profit. You are a mighty sorcerer of all things creative. It's like magic, truly. Every creative thought, vision, and task, no matter how crazy, you hold my hand and say, "Let's do it." I love you with all of my heart. Ann Maloney, you showcased me with your position and words when I first started the entertainment race, extended your kindness, and said my name in a room full of good people. If you call, I'm there. Thank you. Adrienne Rosado, honey, I couldn't have been paired with a better agent. You stood firmly with me and my vision—from the bottom of my heart, thank you. Ann Treistman with Countryman Press, I would say, "You had me at hello," but it was really when you pulled my first cookbook out during our first Zoom meeting. I looked at Chris and said, "I want to work with them." You guys "got it" immediately. No force or convincing needed. You allowed me freedom creatively that no one else would allow. For your belief and support, thank you. Erica Buddington, our connection ignited a fire or two. Thank you for the push to be greater.

To my best friend, my husband, and my manager, Christopher Boudy. On our first date I asked you about your intentions, and you responded without a beat, "I want to marry you, travel with you, and have babies with you." You really meant it all. That's one of the many things that amazes me about you. You do exactly what you say you're going to do, and when you decide you're so sure, so bold and forceful. I agree with my parents, I really met my match. Your flame of ambition is just as big as mine and we always jump in together. If I'm on board with something, you will walk up and map out the ocean. If you have an idea, I can come up with a plan for execution with a solution for every problem.

I admire God's work every time I think of how we got together and how our gifts complement each other's so well. You saw how big my wings were and instead of trying to shove the cage door closed, you dismantled the cage completely in order to love me without limiting me. You never tried to dim my light, you always looked around the room to see what spot would make me shine the brightest.

It's always said that "we're not perfect" when describing ourselves, but I disagree. I feel perfection should be based on your life as an individual and what fits and works for your life and the results you want. With that being said, we're perfect for each other. Whatever issues we have or had helps us iron out wrinkles for some, and admire the depth and contrast for others. What good song doesn't have good highs and deep lows? Doesn't resistance follow every dream closely? Life can be tough, but with you I'll always ask, "What time do I need to show up?" You're my "no matter what." I appreciate you and I love you from here through eternity. I'm yours.

Credits

STYLIST: Mariah Walton Bencik (West London BTQ)

HAIR STYLIST: Rebecca Richardson

NAILS: Bianca Williams "Blessed by Beedy"

MAKEUP: Krystal A. Burrell

FOOD PHOTOGRAPHER: Sam Hanna

FOOD STYLISTS: Toya Boudy and Sam Hanna

CULTURE PHOTOGRAPHER: David Richardson

CREATIVE DIRECTOR AND CO-DIRECTOR: Toya Boudy and Christopher Boudy Sr.

CREATIVE PRODUCER AND CO-PRODUCER: Christopher Boudy Sr. and Toya Boudy

INDEX

A

ahi tuna, Simple Tuna Tartare, 137
allspice seeds, Homemade Seafood
    Boil Seasoning, 85
American cheese, Simple Grilled
    Cheese, 43
anchovy fillets, Beef Tartare, 139
andouille sausage
    Cajun Smothered Potatoes, 167
    Red Beans, 144
    Stove-Top Seafood Boil, 82–84
applewood bacon
    Expensive Ass Deviled Eggs, 139
    Red Beans, 144
    Smothered Okra & Shrimp, 93
artichoke hearts, Spinach and
    Artichoke Grilled Cheese, 44
avocado
    Beef Tartare, 139
    Corn Bread & Black Bean Salsa,
        162–64
    Salmon Tartare, 138
    Simple Tuna Tartare, 137

B

baby scallops, Expensive Ass Deviled
    Eggs, 139
bacon
    Expensive Ass Deviled Eggs, 141
    Liver & Onions, 54
    Oven-Baked Bacon, 15
    Praline Bacon, 189
    Red Beans, 144
    Smothered Okra & Shrimp, 93
Baked Mac & Cheese, 100
bay leaves
    Chicken Noodle Soup, 55
    Homemade Seafood Boil
        Seasoning, 85
Bayou Brunch Po'Boy, 21
BBQ Salmon, 103
BBQ Shrimp, 86
Beef Tartare, 139
beets, Beet Tartare, 138
Beignets with Raspberry Coulis,
    123–24

bell pepper
    Bayou Brunch Po'Boy, 21
    Bloody Mary Shrimp & Grits, 120
    Buttermilk-Roasted Chicken
        with Black Truffle Potatoes,
        129–30
    Collard Greens, 57
    Crab and Crawfish Dressing, 177
    Crawfish Bisque, 158–59
    Eggplant Dressing, 176
    Fried Chicken Kabob, 38
    Jambalaya, 72–73
    Original Dressing Base, 175
    Oyster Dressing, 177
    Red Beans, 144
    Red Gravy, 156
    Seafood Gumbo, 79–81
    Smothered Chicken, 75
    Smothered Okra & Shrimp, 93
    Stuffed Peppers, 170–71
    Succotash, 154
    trinity, 71
Ben's Original rice, Jambalaya, 72–73
beverages
    Hurricane, 217
    Lemonade 4 Ways, 218–19
    Sparkling Punch, 23
biscuits, Drop Biscuits with
    Blackberry Jam, 16–17
black beans, Corn Bread & Black
    Bean Salsa, 162–64
Black Bean Salsa, 162–64
blackberries
    Blackberry Lemonade, 219
    Drop Biscuits with Blackberry
        Jam, 16–17
black-eyed peas, Black-Eyed Peas &
    Collard Greens, 182–83
black truffle mayo
    Expensive Ass Deviled Eggs, 139
    black truffle potatoes, Buttermilk-
        Roasted Chicken with Black
        Truffle Potatoes, 129–30
    Bloody Mary Shrimp & Grits, 120
bourbon
    Bourbon Brown Sugar Spiral Ham,
        180
    Bourbon-Glazed Lamp Chops with

        Marinated Beans, 193–95
bread crumbs
    Crab and Crawfish Dressing, 177
    Crawfish Bisque, 158–59
    Eggplant Parmesan, 30–31
    Fried Ravioli with Tasso Cream,
        116
    Oyster Dressing, 177
    Stuffed Peppers, 170–71
    See also panko bread crumbs
bread pudding, White Chocolate
    Bread Pudding, 211–13
breakfast sausage
    Eggplant Dressing, 176
    Stuffed Peppers, 170–71
Brioche hamburger buns, Shrimp on
    Bun, 37
Browned Butter Scallops, 127
buttermilk
    Buttermilk-Roasted Chicken
        with Black Truffle Potatoes,
        129–30
    Buttermilk Turkey Wings, 41
    Fried Chicken, 96
    Fried Chicken & Watermelon Jam
        Sandwich, 48–49
    Fried Fish, 95
    Fried Okra, 153
    Fried Shrimp & Rocafella Cream,
        68–70
    Shrimp on Bun, 37
butters, Compound Butters, 150

C

Cajun Corn on the Cob, 148
Cajun Smothered Potatoes, 167
cannellini beans, Bourbon-Glazed
    Lamp Chops with Marinated
    Beans, 193–95
capers
    Beef Tartare, 139
    Crab Cakes with Lemon Caper
        Cream, 134–35
carrots
    Chicken Noodle Soup, 55
    trinity, 71
catfish, Fried Fish, 95

caviar
    Expensive Ass Deviled Eggs, 139
    Expensive Ass Salad, 131–33
celery
    Bayou Brunch Po'Boy, 21
    Bloody Mary Shrimp & Grits, 120
    Chicken Noodle Soup, 55
    Chicken Salad, 46
    Collard Greens, 57
    Crab and Crawfish Dressing, 177
    Crawfish Bisque, 158–59
    Eggplant Dressing, 176
    Jambalaya, 72–73
    Original Dressing Base, 175
    Oyster Dressing, 177
    Red Beans, 144
    Red Gravy, 156
    Seafood Gumbo, 79–81
    Smothered Chicken, 75
    Stove-Top Seafood Boil, 82–84
    Stuffed Peppers, 170–71
    Succotash, 154
    trinity, 71
celery seeds, Homemade Seafood
    Boil Seasoning, 85
champagne, Expensive Ass Salad,
    131–33
Chardonnay, Original Lemonade,
    218
Chargrilled Oysters with Blue
    Crabmeat, 89
Cheddar
    Baked Mac & Cheese, 100
    Crawfish Grilled Cheese, 43–44
cheese
    Baked Mac & Cheese, 100
    Chargrilled Oysters with Blue
      Crabmeat, 89–90
    Eggplant Parmesan, 30–31
    Endive Appetizers, 186
    French Fries 4 Ways, 58–60
    Garlic Parmesan Butter, 150
    Grilled Cheese 4 Ways, 42–45
    Lemon Pepper Green Beans, 166
    Oyster Dressing, 178
    Pepperoni Lasagna, 62–64
    See also cream cheese
cherry tomatoes
    Black-Eyed Peas & Collard Greens,
      182–83
    Bloody Mary Shrimp & Grits, 120
    Corn Bread & Black Bean Salsa,
      163–65
    Ravioli, 99
chicken, Fried Chicken, 96

chicken, whole, Buttermilk-Roasted
    Chicken with Black Truffle
    Potatoes, 129–30
chicken breasts
    Chicken Noodle Soup, 55
    Chicken Salad, 46
    Fried Chicken Kabob, 38
    Jambalaya, 72–73
    Seafood Gumbo, 79–81
    Smothered Chicken, 75
chicken livers, Liver & Onions, 54
chicken thighs
    Christmas Chicken, 173
    Fried Chicken & Watermelon Jam
      Sandwich, 48–49
chives
    Expensive Ass Deviled Eggs, 139
    Salmon Tartare, 138
chocolate
    Strawberry Shortcake, 201–3
    White Chocolate Bread Pudding,
      211–13
Christmas Chicken, 173
chuck or eye of round roast,
    Yakamein, 103
cilantro
    Beef Tartare, 139
    Corn Bread & Black Bean Salsa,
      163–65
    Simple Tuna Tartare, 137
    Sweet Potato Bisque, 160–61
cinnamon
    Beignets with Raspberry Coulis,
      123–24
    Perfect Cup of Coffee, 19
    Praline Sweet Potatoes with
      Whiskey Mallo Cream, 190
    Pumpkin Roll, 205–6
Cinnamon Butter, 150
Citrus Lemonade, 219
Classic Steak & Lobster, 114–15
cloves, Homemade Seafood Boil
    Seasoning, 85
coconut, Coconut Shrimp with
    Mango Chili Sauce, 107–8
coffee grounds, Perfect Cup of
    Coffee, 19
collard greens, 185
    Black-Eyed Peas & Collard Greens,
      182–83
    Collard Greens, 57
commodity foods, 25
Compound Butters, 150
cookies, Peanut Butter Cookies, 27
Cookies & Cream Ice Cream, 199–200

coriander seeds, Homemade Seafood
    Boil Seasoning, 85
corn
    Cajun Corn on the Cob, 148
    Corn Bread & Black Bean Salsa,
      162–64
    Stove-Top Seafood Boil, 82–84
    Sweet Potato Bisque, 160–61
corn bread
    Black-Eyed Peas & Collard Greens,
      182–83
    Crab and Crawfish Dressing, 177
    Eggplant Dressing, 176
    Original Dressing Base, 175
    Oyster Dressing, 177
Corn Bread, 147
Corn Bread & Black Bean Salsa,
    162–64
crab
    Crab and Crawfish Dressing, 177
    Stove-Top Seafood Boil, 82–84
crab legs, Seafood Gumbo, 79–81
crabmeat
    Crab and Crawfish Dressing, 177
    Crab Cakes with Lemon Caper
      Cream, 134–35
crabs, gumbo, Seafood Gumbo, 79–81
cranberries, Christmas Chicken, 173
crawfish, crawfish tails
    Bayou Brunch Po'Boy, 21
    Crab and Crawfish Dressing, 177
    Crawfish Bisque, 158–59
    Crawfish Grilled Cheese, 43–44
    Seafood Gumbo, 79–81
cream cheese, Baked Mac & Cheese,
    100
Crème de la Crème Grilled Cheese,
    45
cream of wheat (farina), 10
Crème de la Crème Grilled Cheese,
    45
cubed toasted bread, Original
    Dressing Base, 175

D

dark rum, Hurricane, 217
Dijon mustard
    Beef Tartare, 139
    Crab Cakes with Lemon Caper
      Cream, 134–35
    Expensive Ass Deviled Eggs, 139
dill pickle relish, Potato Salad, 162
dill seeds, Homemade Seafood Boil
    Seasoning, 85

Double Stuf Oreos, Cookies & Cream Ice Cream, 199–200
dressings
    Crab and Crawfish Dressing, 177
    Dressing 4 Ways, 174–78
    Eggplant Dressing, 176
    Expensive Ass Salad, 133
    Original Dressing Base, 175
    Oyster Dressing, 178
    Potato Salad, 162
Drop Biscuits with Blackberry Jam, 16–17

E

edible gold
    Expensive Ass Deviled Eggs, 139
    Expensive Ass Salad, 131–33
egg noodles, Chicken Noodle Soup, 55
eggplant
    Eggplant Dressing, 176
    Eggplant Parmesan, 30–31
eggs
    Bayou Brunch Po'Boy, 21
    Beef Tartare, 139
    Chicken Salad, 46
    Coconut Shrimp with Mango Chili Sauce, 107–8
    Crawfish Bisque, 158–59
    Eggplant Parmesan, 30–31
    Eggs & Rice, 34
    Expensive Ass Deviled Eggs, 141
    Fried Ravioli with Tasso Cream, 116
    Fried Shrimp & Rocafella Cream, 68–70
    Lavender Tea Cakes, 214
    Lemon Squares, 28
    Pancetta Pancakes, 119
    Peach Cobbler, 210
    Pepperoni Lasagna, 62–64
    The Perfect Scramble, 13
    Potato Salad, 162
    Pumpkin Roll, 205–6
    7Up Cake, 208
    Strawberry Shortcake, 201–3
    White Chocolate Bread Pudding, 211–13
    Yakamein, 103
Eggs & Rice, 34
elbow noodles, Baked Mac & Cheese, 100
Emily Taught Me, 65
endives, Endive Appetizers, 186

Expensive Ass Deviled Eggs, 139
Expensive Ass Salad, 131–33

F

fish fry, 94–95
French bread
    Bayou Brunch Po'Boy, 21
    BBQ Shrimp, 86
    White Chocolate Bread Pudding, 211–13
french fries
    Beef Tartare, 139
    French Fries 4 Ways, 58–60
Fried Chicken, 96
Fried Chicken Kabob, 38
Fried Chicken & Watermelon Jam Sandwich, 48–49
Fried Fish, 95
Fried Okra, 153
Fried Ravioli with Tasso Cream, 116
Fried Shrimp & Rocafella Cream, 68–70

G

garlic
    Baked Mac & Cheese, 100
    BBQ Shrimp, 86
    Black-Eyed Peas & Collard Greens, 182–83
    Bloody Mary Shrimp & Grits, 120
    Bourbon-Glazed Lamp Chops with Marinated Beans, 193–95
    Browned Butter Scallops, 127
    Buttermilk-Roasted Chicken with Black Truffle Potatoes, 129–30
    Buttermilk Turkey Wings, 41
    Cajun Corn on the Cob, 148
    Cajun Smothered Potatoes, 167
    Chargrilled Oysters with Blue Crabmeat, 89–90
    Chicken Noodle Soup, 55
    Christmas Chicken, 173
    Classic Steak & Lobster, 114–15
    Collard Greens, 57
    Crab and Crawfish Dressing, 177
    Crab Cakes with Lemon Caper Cream, 134–35
    Crawfish Bisque, 158–59
    Crawfish Grilled Cheese, 43
    Crème de la Crème Grilled Cheese, 45

Eggplant Dressing, 176
    French Fries 4 Ways, 58–60
    Fried Chicken, 96
    Fried Ravioli with Tasso Cream, 116
    Fried Shrimp & Rocafella Cream, 68–70
    Jambalaya, 73–74
    Lemon Pepper Green Beans, 166
    Original Dressing Base, 175
    Oyster Dressing, 178
    Pepperoni Lasagna, 62–64
    Ravioli, 99
    Red Beans, 144
    Red Gravy, 156
    Seafood Gumbo, 79–81
    Smothered Chicken, 75
    Smothered Okra & Shrimp, 93
    Spinach and Artichoke Grilled Cheese, 44
    Stove-Top Seafood Boil, 82–84
    Stuffed Peppers, 170–71
    Succotash, 154
    Sweet Potato Bisque, 160–61
Garlic Parmesan Butter, 150
ginger
    Beet Tartare, 138
    Simple Tuna Tartare, 137
goat cheese, Endive Appetizers, 186
gravy
    French Fries 4 Ways, 58–60
    Red Gravy, 156
    See also roux
green beans, Lemon Pepper Green Beans, 166
green onions
    Beet Tartare, 138
    Black-Eyed Peas & Collard Greens, 182–83
    Crab and Crawfish Dressing, 177
    Crawfish Bisque, 158–59
    Crawfish Grilled Cheese, 43–44
    Eggs & Rice, 34
    Fried Ravioli with Tasso Cream, 116
    Jambalaya, 72–73
    Original Dressing Base, 175
    Oyster Dressing, 177
    Red Beans, 144
    Stove-Top Seafood Boil, 82–84
    Sweet Potato Bisque, 160–61
grenadine, Hurricane, 217
Grilled Cheese 4 Ways, 42–45
grits
    Bloody Mary Shrimp & Grits, 120
    Southern Grits, 14

ground beef
    Pepperoni Lasagna, 62–64
    Stuffed Peppers, 170–71
ground breakfast sausage, Stuffed
    Peppers, 170–71
ground red pepper, Homemade
    Seafood Boil Seasoning, 85
gumbo, Seafood Gumbo, 79–81

H

ham, cubed, Succotash, 154
ham, spiral, Bourbon Brown Sugar
    Spiral Ham, 180
hard-boiled eggs
    Chicken Salad, 46
    Expensive Ass Deviled Eggs, 139
    Potato Salad, 162
    Yakamein, 103
hash, Sweet Potato Bisque, 160–61
heavy cream
    Cajun Smothered Potatoes, 167
    Crab Cakes with Lemon Caper
        Cream, 134–35
    Fried Ravioli with Tasso Cream, 116
    Lemon Caper Cream, 135
    Sweet Potato Bisque, 160–61
    White Chocolate Bread Pudding,
        211–13
Homemade Coffee Syrup, 19
Homemade Seafood Boil Seasoning, 85
hot sausage
    Bayou Brunch Po'Boy, 21
    Seafood Gumbo, 79–81
Hurricane, 217

I

Italian bread crumbs
    Fried Ravioli with Tasso Cream, 116
    Stuffed Peppers, 170–71
Italian sausage, Pepperoni Lasagna,
    62–64

J

jalapeño
    Beet Tartare, 138
    Simple Tuna Tartare, 137
Jambalaya, 72–73
Jimmy Dean sausage
    Crab and Crawfish Dressing, 177
    Original Dressing Base, 175
    Oyster Dressing, 177
    Stuffed Peppers, 170–71

K

kabobs, Fried Chicken Kabob, 38

L

lamb loin chops, Bourbon-Glazed
    Lamp Chops with Marinated
    Beans, 193–95
lasagna noodles, Pepperoni Lasagna,
    62–64
Lavender Tea Cakes, 214
lemon
    BBQ Salmon, 104
    BBQ Shrimp, 86
    Blackberry Jam, 17
    Buttermilk-Roasted Chicken
        with Black Truffle Potatoes,
        129–30
    Christmas Chicken, 173
    Citrus Lemonade, 219
    Crab Cakes with Lemon Caper
        Cream, 134–35
    Expensive Ass Deviled Eggs, 139
    Expensive Ass Salad, 131–33
    Fried Chicken & Watermelon Jam
        Sandwich, 48–49
    Lemonade 4 Ways, 218–19
    Lemon Caper Cream, 135
    Lemon Pepper Butter, 150
    Lemon Pepper Green Beans, 166
    Lemon Squares, 28
    Salmon Tartare, 138
    Stove-Top Seafood Boil, 82–84
lima beans, Succotash, 154
lime
    Beef Tartare, 139
    Black-Eyed Peas & Collard Greens,
        182–83
    Collard Greens, 57
    Corn Bread & Black Bean Salsa,
        162–64
    Hurricane, 217
    Salmon Tartare, 138
    Simple Tuna Tartare, 137
    Strawberry Lemonade, 219
Liver & Onions, 54
lobster tails
    Classic Steak & Lobster, 114–15
    Expensive Ass Salad, 131–33
lump blue crabmeat, Chargrilled
    Oysters with Blue Crabmeat, 89
lump crabmeat
    Crab Cakes with Lemon Caper
        Cream, 134–35

Expensive Ass Deviled Eggs, 139
Expensive Ass Salad, 131–33
Stuffed Peppers, 170–71

M

marinara sauce, Eggplant Parmesan,
    30–31
marinated beans, Bourbon-Glazed
    Lamp Chops with Marinated
    Beans, 193–95
marjoram, Homemade Seafood Boil
    Seasoning, 85
marshmallow fluff, Praline Sweet
    Potatoes with Whiskey Mallo
    Cream, 190
mayonnaise
    Chicken Salad, 46
    Crab Cakes with Lemon Caper
        Cream, 134–35
    Potato Salad, 162
    Simple Grilled Cheese, 43
mirepoix, 71
mozzarella
    Crème de la Crème Grilled
        Cheese, 45
    Eggplant Parmesan, 30–31
    Pepperoni Lasagna, 62–64
    Spinach and Artichoke Grilled
        Cheese, 44
mustard, Dijon
    Beef Tartare, 139
    Crab Cakes with Lemon Caper
        Cream, 134–35
    Expensive Ass Deviled Eggs,
        141
mustard, yellow, Potato Salad,
    162
mustard seeds, Homemade Seafood
    Boil Seasoning, 85

N

new potatoes
    Potato Salad, 162
    Stove-Top Seafood Boil, 82–84
New York strip steaks, Classic Steak
    & Lobster, 114–15

O

okra
    Fried Okra, 153
    Smothered Okra & Shrimp, 93
    Succotash, 154

onion
    Bayou Brunch Po'Boy, 21
    BBQ Shrimp, 86
    Black-Eyed Peas & Collard Greens, 182–83
    Bloody Mary Shrimp & Grits, 120
    Buttermilk-Roasted Chicken with Black Truffle Potatoes, 129–30
    Chicken Noodle Soup, 55
    Collard Greens, 57
    Crab and Crawfish Dressing, 177
    Crawfish Bisque, 158–59
    Eggplant Dressing, 176
    Fried Chicken Kabob, 38
    Fried Shrimp & Rocafella Cream, 68–70
    Liver & Onions, 54
    Original Dressing Base, 175
    Oyster Dressing, 177
    Pepperoni Lasagna, 62–64
    Red Beans, 144
    Seafood Gumbo, 79–81
    Simple Tuna Tartare, 137
    Smothered Chicken, 75
    Smothered Okra & Shrimp, 93
    Stuffed Peppers, 170–71
    Sweet Potato Bisque, 160–61
    trinity, 71
    See also green onions
onion, red
    Beef Tartare, 139
    Corn Bread & Black Bean Salsa, 163–65
onion, sweet
    Fried Ravioli with Tasso Cream, 116
    Red Gravy, 156
    Stove-Top Seafood Boil, 82–84
    Succotash, 154
onion, white
    Ravioli, 99
    Simple Tuna Tartare, 137
onion, yellow, Jambalaya, 72–73
orange
    Citrus Lemonade, 219
    Hurricane, 217
    Stove-Top Seafood Boil, 82–84
Original Dressing Base, 175
Original Lemonade, 218
Oven-Baked Bacon, 15
Oyster Dressing, 177
oysters, jar of, Oyster Dressing, 177
oysters in a shell, Chargrilled Oysters with Blue Crabmeat, 89

P

pancakes, Pancetta Pancakes, 119
panko bread crumbs
    Classic Steak & Lobster, 114–15
    Coconut Shrimp with Mango Chili Sauce, 107–8
    Crab Cakes with Lemon Caper Cream, 134–35
    Stuffed Peppers, 170–71
Parmesan cheese
    Chargrilled Oysters with Blue Crabmeat, 89
    Compound Butters, 150
    Eggplant Parmesan, 30–31
    French Fries 4 Ways, 60
    Lemon Pepper Green Beans, 166
    Oyster Dressing, 177
    Pepperoni Lasagna, 62–64
passion fruit juice, Hurricane, 217
pastry ring mold, Salmon Tartare, 138
Patton's hot sausage patties, Bayou Brunch Po'Boy, 21
peaches, Peach Cobbler, 210
peanut butter
    commodity foods, 25
    Peanut Butter Cookies, 27
pecans
    Endive Appetizers, 186
    Praline Bacon, 189
    Praline Sweet Potatoes with Whiskey Mallo Cream, 190
pepper Jack
    Baked Mac & Cheese, 100
    Crawfish Grilled Cheese, 43–44
    Spinach and Artichoke Grilled Cheese, 44
Pepperoni Lasagna, 62–64
Perfect Cup of Coffee, 19
The Perfect Scramble, 13
pickle relish
    Chicken Salad, 46
    dill, in Potato Salad, 162
potatoes
    Buttermilk-Roasted Chicken with Black Truffle Potatoes, 129–30
    Cajun Smothered Potatoes, 167
    French Fries 4 Ways, 58–60
    Potato Salad, 162
    Stove-Top Seafood Boil, 82–84
    sweet, Praline Sweet Potatoes with Whiskey Mallo Cream, 190
    sweet, Sweet Potato Bisque, 160–61
Praline Bacon, 189
Praline Sweet Potatoes with Whiskey Mallo Cream, 190
prime beef tenderloin, Beef Tartare, 139
prosciutto, Black-Eyed Peas & Collard Greens, 182–83
prosecco wine
    Bourbon-Glazed Lamp Chops with Marinated Beans, 193–95
    Endive Appetizers, 186
provolone
    Crème de la Crème Grilled Cheese, 45
    Spinach and Artichoke Grilled Cheese, 44
pumpkin, canned, Pumpkin Roll, 205–6

R

raspberries, Beignets with Raspberry Coulis, 123–24
ravioli
    Fried Ravioli with Tasso Cream, 116
    Ravioli, 99
red beans, dried, Red Beans, 144
Red Gravy, 156
red onion
    Beef Tartare, 139
    Corn Bread & Black Bean Salsa, 162–64
rice
    Crawfish Bisque, 158–59
    Eggs & Rice, 34
    Jambalaya, 75
    Red Beans, 144
    Seafood Gumbo, 79–81
    Smothered Chicken, 75
    Smothered Okra & Shrimp, 93
    Succotash, 154
ricotta cheese, Pepperoni Lasagna, 62–64
roux, 76–78
rum
    Hurricane, 217
    White Chocolate Bread Pudding, 211–13
russet potatoes
    French Fries 4 Ways, 58–60
    Potato Salad, 162

S

salmon fillets
    BBQ Salmon, 103
    Salmon Tartare, 138
sausage, andouille
    Cajun Smothered Potatoes, 167
    Red Beans, 144
    Stove-Top Seafood Boil, 82–84
sausage, breakfast
    Eggplant Dressing, 176
    Stuffed Peppers, 170–71
sausage, hot
    Bayou Brunch Po'Boy, 21
    Seafood Gumbo, 79–81
sausage, Italian, Pepperoni Lasagna, 62–64
sausage, Jimmy Dean
    Crab and Crawfish Dressing, 177
    Original Dressing Base, 175
    Oyster Dressing, 177
    Stuffed Peppers, 170–71
sausage, links
    Seafood Gumbo, 79–81
    Stove-Top Seafood Boil, 82–84
sausage, smoked
    Fried Chicken Kabob, 37
    Jambalaya, 72–73
scallops
    Browned Butter Scallops, 127
    Expensive Ass Deviled Eggs, 141
    Expensive Ass Salad, 131–33
Seafood Gumbo, 79–81
7Up Cake, 208
shortcake, Strawberry Shortcake, 201–3
shrimp
    Bayou Brunch Po'Boy, 21
    BBQ Shrimp, 86
    Bloody Mary Shrimp & Grits, 120
    Coconut Shrimp with Mango Chili Sauce, 107–8
    Fried Shrimp & Rocafella Cream, 68–70
    Jambalaya, 72–73
    Seafood Gumbo, 79–81
    Shrimp on Bun, 37
    Smothered Okra & Shrimp, 93

Stove-Top Seafood Boil, 82–84
Succotash, 154
Simple Grilled Cheese, 43
Simple Tuna Tartare, 137–39
smoked sausage
    Fried Chicken Kabob, 38
    Jambalaya, 72–73
Smoky Feta Crumble Butter, 150
Smothered Chicken, 75
Smothered Okra & Shrimp, 93
sour cream
    Baked Mac & Cheese, 100
    Strawberry Shortcake, 201–3
Southern Grits, 14
spaghetti, Yakamein, 103
Sparkling Punch, 23
Spinach and Artichoke Grilled Cheese, 44
Spinach Cream Sauce, 68–70
spiral ham, Bourbon Brown Sugar Spiral Ham, 180
Spring mix salad greens, Expensive Ass Salad, 131–33
Stove-Top Seafood Boil, 82–84
strawberries
    Sparkling Punch, 23
    Strawberry Lemonade, 219
    Strawberry Shortcake, 201–3
Stuffed Peppers, 170–71
Succotash, 154
Sweet Baby Ray's Barbecue Sauce, BBQ Salmon, 103
Sweet Cream Farina, 10
sweet Italian sausage, Pepperoni Lasagna, 62–64
sweet potatoes
    Praline Sweet Potatoes with Whiskey Mallo Cream, 190
    Sweet Potato Bisque, 160–61
Swiss, Crème de la Crème Grilled Cheese, 45

T

Tartare 4 Ways, 137–39
tasso, Fried Ravioli with Tasso Cream, 116
Texas toast bread, Grilled Cheese 4 Ways, 42–45
toast points, Beef Tartare, 139

tomatoes
    Black-Eyed Peas & Collard Greens, 182–83
    Bloody Mary Shrimp & Grits, 120
    Corn Bread & Black Bean Salsa, 162–64
    Jambalaya, 72–73
    Pepperoni Lasagna, 62–64
    The Perfect Scramble, 13
    Ravioli, 99
    Red Gravy, 156
    Smothered Okra & Shrimp, 93
    Succotash, 154
turkey neck, Red Beans, 144
turkey wings, Buttermilk Turkey Wings, 41

V

vodka
    Bloody Mary Shrimp & Grits, 120

W

watermelon, 51
    Fried Chicken & Watermelon Jam Sandwich, 48–49
    Watermelon Jam, 48–49
whiskey, Praline Sweet Potatoes with Whiskey Mallo Cream, 190
white chocolate
    White Chocolate Bread Pudding, 211–13
    White Chocolate Sauce, 213
white rum, Hurricane, 217

Y

Yakamein, 103
yellow cornmeal
    Corn Bread, 147
    Corn Bread & Black Bean Salsa, 163–65
    Fried Fish, 219
    Fried Okra, 153
yellow mustard, Potato Salad, 162
yellow onions, Jambalaya, 219
Yukon Gold potatoes, Buttermilk-Roasted Chicken with Black Truffle Potatoes, 129–30